Urantia Book Programming

Urantia Book Programming
by
Troy R. Bishop

Published by CreateSpace
© 2017 Troy R. Bishop
Printed in the United States of America

1 3 5 7 9 0 8 6 4 2

First Edition, 2017

ISBN-10: 1977833497
ISBN-13: 978-1977833495

Cover and art by Troy R. Bishop

Contents

5. Paradigm

Protocol

6. Libraries

Code Libraries

1

Introduction

Background

Scope

This is a reference manual for IT professionals.

It describes an information technology, referred to as *The Urantia Book Programming Paradigm (UBPP)*, or simply *Urantia Book Programming (UBP)*, which is used to manipulate Urantia Book textual data.

The Urantia Book Programming Paradigm consists of *The Urantia Book Programming Protocol (UBPR)* and *The Urantia Book Programming Language (UBPL)*.

UBP programs consist of components specified in the Urantia Book Programming Protocol; namely, the program code itself, in conjunction with special plain text files, called *exemplar files*, of Urantia Book text, and special plain-text files of numerical data, called *metrics files*, which describe *The Urantia Book*'s structure.

The information contained in these pages can also be of use in the areas of management and support. Particularly helpful in these areas may be the included narration of the developmental history of UBP, describing, as it does, the reasons behind certain technical decisions made in the formative years of Urantia Book-related IT—that is, of UBP.

Timeline

On January 1, 2006, the English text of *The Urantia Book* entered the public domain, and on that same day I began the development of *Urantia Book Explorer*, the first Urantia Book browser, which I completed in May, 2007. Other programs followed.

All together, this effort produced the following:

- *Urantia Book Explorer* (January 2006 to May 2007).

- *The Multilingual Urantia Book* (the *Polygloss*) (June 2007 to November 2007).

- *Urantia Book Translator* (December 2007 to January 2009).

- The *UBDS*, or *Urantia Book Data System* (December 2007 to January 2009).

- *UBSearch* (May 2012).

- *Urantia Book Views* (November 2012).

- *Urantia Book Access*, (for mobile Android devices) (November 2015).

During this time, I was perfecting a technique specifically designed for processing Urantia Book text, an approach that I have named *exemplar metrics*.

Exemplar metrics is the engine that drives Urantia Book Programming.

Upon completing Urantia Book Translator, I offered Urantia Book Translator free to the Urantia Foundation. Some members of Urantia Foundation were interested and suggested that they employ Urantia Book Transalator for their translations, but ultimately that suggestion was not approved.

Upon completing the UBDS, I prepared video tutorials and documentation for the UBDS, which, at the current time, are located at

https://www.facebook.com/UrantiaBookProgramming/

and are also located, on a permanent basis, at

https://archive.org/details/@troy_r_bishop

(Because of bandwidth considerations, videos at the latter site, the Internet Archive, must be downloaded and viewed locally or uploaded elsewhere.)

At this point, the Urantia Book Programming Paradigm, which had been developing with each successive item on the timeline above, was complete. Its components, the Urantia Book Programming Protocol and the Urantia Book Programming Language, were fully formed and in service.

UBP Instances

Some notable uses to which Urantia Book Programming has been put and events that have affected UBP since its development include the following:

• Tigran Aivazian, of London, England, has been applying exemplar metrics on a case by case basis in his publishing of Urantia Books and Urantia Book derivatives in various forms and installing them in key hubs of the cyberworld. He designed, produced, and published *The British Study Edition of The Urantia Papers*, including critical apparatus, using exemplar metrics to check its finished makeup. He used these same methods to publish and on-demand print *The Guardian Plates*, a photoreplica of the first printing of *The Urantia Book* whose images were scanned and arranged by an anonymous group, who placed the images and their collection in the public domain.

• In 2010, over a period of several months, I downloaded and converted to exemplars all then existing language versions of *The Urantia Book* from Urantia Foundation for my own use. Soon after, Urantia Foundation developed a need for a complete new set of master files of the text of *The Urantia Book* in all the languages that had been published, including English. Working in collaboration, a) Tigran Aivazian, b) Urantia Society of Greater New York (USGNY), c) Urantia Foundation (Larry Watkins), and d) myself produced, for Urantia Foundation, a collection of all of the files for all of all the then current languages, from my collection of exemplar files.

• July, 2011—USGNY opted for the use of Urantia Book Translator for their then upcoming translation of *The Urantia Book* into the Turkish language. This Urantia Book Translator-assisted translation was completed and published.

• USGNY developed and made available the following exemplar-metrics based software:

    1. UBSE5 classic search engine.

    2. SmartAid, exemplar-based search engine, including translations in 22 languages.

    3. UBSS Urantia Book Super Search - exemplar based search engine, including translations in 22 languages.

• USGNY plans to add a feature devoted to exemplar metrics to the Technology Center at their website.

Development Stages of UBP

For the creation of Urantia Book Explorer, it was necessary to extract certain structural information from then existing Urantia Book text files. For example, a two-dimensional count, in machine-readable form, of the number of sections in each paper of *The Urantia Book*, and for each of those sections, the number of paragraphs it contains.

This was accomplished by writing and executing a number of matching and analysis programs, using Urantia Book text files as input. These programs, written in the PHP programming language, were for one-time use only.

Urantia Book Programming (UBP) had its horizons widened during the Multilingual Urantia Book project, during the task of deriving the data that was subsequently data-designed as the *Urantia Book Metrics (UBM)*. These data were derived from Urantia Book files by analyzing the Urantia Book files by means of writing and executing utility programs in PHP and PERL. The resulting data identify—for each *computer line* (every sequential portion of text terminated by CRLF, not to be confused with *grammatical sentences*)—of text in *The Urantia Book* a *textual unit designation code*. Each textual unit designation code identifies one of the following: a paper number within *The Urantia Book*, a section number within a paper, or a paragraph number within a section. Thus was defined and created a full set of textual identification numbers for each of 4 separate then existing line designation systems:

1. Urantia Foundation (*ufn*), referred to as *SRT* numbers

2. Urantia Book Fellowship (*ubf*)

3. Absolute (abs)

4. Second Society Foundation (*ssf*)

In addition to introducing the use of Urantia Book Metrics, the Multilingual Urantia Book project introduced a number of language neutral protocols. These protocols, which are now a part of the Urantia Book Programming Protocol, include, for example, the use of unicode and the storage of various translations of *The Urantia Book* in distilled form, called *Urantia Book Exemplars (UBE)*, that can be shaped, through the programmatic application of Urantia Book metrics parameters, into particular desired formats or media.

Urantia Book Programming was further advanced in the Urantia Book Translator project, which fine tuned the Urantia Book Programming protocols by standardizing the number of lines in each of the 197 Urantia Book exemplar files. These numbers thus became invariant, the same fixed numbers for a given paper no matter what the language.

From this fixed numericity came the total correspondence, on a line-by-line basis, of all lines in a given paper across all languages, whose descripions of each line thus became the genome, if you will, of *The Urantia Book*. And from this language-independent line correspondence came the ability to standardize the processing, formatting, conversion, and other manipulations of the Urantia Book exemplar files on a batch, or total book, basis, by programmatic means.

The subsequent development of Urantia Book Codifier brought about the integration of Urantia Book Translator and Urantia Book Codifier into a single functional system, the *Urantia Book Data System (UBDS)*, whose component subsystems were thus empowed with the capability of central processing, conversion, and storage and retrieval capabilities, as well as with far-reaching potentials for application and service.

Capabilities

Multiforming

The tools of Urantia Book Programming can convert stored exemplar files (distilled Urantia Book files) of any language into outputs for various media. For example, a 45-second run of Urantia Book Codifier can convert a particular language's exemplar files into a full set of 197 files—web pages—fully formatted for the web.

UBP programs can produce lists of the papers—number and title—of *The Urantia Book* by a batch run executed on full sets of exemplar files.

UBP programs can convert exemplar files into formats of various styles including, for example, setting apart ordered lists by inserting blank lines before and after each list or by labeling only the first line in each list. These UBP programs make the appropriate decisions for each line in *The Urantia Book* from input metrics files created to specify these variables.

UBP programs can apply paragraph designation codes to the paragraphs in *The Urantia Book* in any language and using any paragraph designation scheme through the use of specially prepared input metrics files.

UBP programs can convert exemplar files into special-purpose files for various purposes. For example, in the future, when written in a compiled language that incorporates the necessary capabilities, including full unicode support, UBP programs could prepare files that would be ready for upload to the print-on-demand sales facilities of Amazon.com.

UBP programs could be written to extract certain passages from Urantia Book exemplar files, for example, for pamphlets. They could do this in any exemplarized and metricized language and further, they could format those extracted passages in a style, graphical layout, and print format required by a print shop.

UBP programs can be used as applications (programs), as is the case with Urantia Book Translator, Urantia Book Explorer, The Multilingual Urantia Book, and Urantia Book Codifier.

Analysis

UBP programs can extract metrics information from metrics files to create new metrics files with derivative information that is implicit, but not explicit, in the original metrics files.

UBP programs can analyze exemplar files and other UBP files, such as working files (translated files in the process of being created) and reference files (translated files already finalized), for certain flaws—for example, for an incorrect number of physical lines (not computer lines) in one or more section titles (not in the section body itself). Section title line breaks are supposed to match the line breaks of the 1955 first printing of the English language Urantia Book.

UBP programs could compare the contents of different copies of the alleged same exemplar files. These comparisons would have to incorporate a standardization of spacing within the program; for example, perhaps copying the files and removing all spaces between and within words. They would also have to normalize italics for the comparison, since italics in two files can be rendered as apparently identical to the human eye but actually contain different markup beneath the rendering.

As an example, who would normally know whether, in a document that he or she may have prepared, the spaces within or at the end of a particular run of italicized text were themselves in italics? Or whether an apparent italicized run might perhaps be a concatenation of two or more italic runs? The human eye doesn't care, but the comparison program, which deals with the markup for the comparison, does. Therefore the italicization would have to be normalized, at least on an interim basis, in a comparison copy.

Data Management

UBP programs can derive UBP files from regular online files and documents. For example, UBP programs can extract a file specifying the script (set of characters), necessary to translate unicode-encoded documents into any specific language, by assembling any huge file in that language (concatenations of general books and articles) and extracting from it a file listing the individual characters encountered in it.

Similarly, UBP programs can be used to process data in standard ways; for example, to process the world database of unicode characters and their attributes (as maintained by the Unicode Consortium, at www.unicode.org), in order to create a unicode dictionary that could be used as a lookup table in a UBP program that would use the list of unicode characters for a particular language as derived above.

UBP programs can be used to manage data banks of Urantia Book files.

UBP programs can also be used as utility programs to carry out tasks that arise in the course of Urantia Book Programming.

2

Basics

Paradigm

Pre-Urantia Book Explorer Data Processing

EACH emerging program in the group comprising the Urantia Book Data System was developed at a different stage in the evolution of the Urantia Book Programming Paradigm. The evolution of the paradigm occurred primarily because the program requirements grew to encompass greater and more diverse functionality with each succeeding program.

The accruing and sometimes changing elements of the Urantia Book Programming Paradigm for each sequentially emerging program are described here, in the order in which they were developed, as a reference for IT professionals who might evaluate, revisit, or maintain these applications.

As mentioned earlier, in order to develop the first project—Urantia Book Explorer—it was necessary to process sets of Urantia Book text files and extract structural information from them.

The data processing platform used was a PC. The data processing operating system was Windows XP.

PHP4 was chosen as the data processing language. A

scripting language was chosen instead of a compiled language because of the informal fluidity of script compared with the formal regulation of compiled languages and also because interpreters are usually free, where compilers were expensive. PHP4 would be able to facilitate file reading and writing and data manipulation. On the down side, PHP4 was a command-line, console interpreter with no Windows GUI, which thus required the programmer to deal with relatively primitive methods of using it.

The plan for data extraction was to progressively extract and refine data by successively writing and executing a series of data extraction programs, data checking programs, and data analysis programs, which, in some instances, had to be altered for each succeeding program execution. Sometimes manual data correction was used on outputted data, and sometimes targeted programmatic, data corrections were used, where the output processing reports indicated that they should be used—for example, to inject a missing space into one specific line of text between two words.

Urantia Book Explorer Development

It was planned that Urantia Book Explorer would take the form of a scripted web page consisting of a cluster of frames into which to load and control selectable web pages of the Urantia Book. By embodying this approach, Urantia Book Explorer would have access to the *dynamic* display capabilities of its host web browser.

Microsoft Internet Explorer was selected as the web browser, with Microsoft Windows as its host Operating system, each of them at that time having over 90% of the world usage share, hence likely being able to serve the largest portion of then-future UBDS users.

There would be no cross-browser coding.

To achieve dynamic data display and manipulation, the final roll call of programming languages and tools with which to create Urantia Book Explorer would be:

1. HTML

2. CSS

3. JavaScript

4. The Microsoft Document Object Model (DOM).

JavaScript was chosen over a compiled language to make the system as easy as possible for those who would come later to understand and maintain. And because, as I mentioned in the previous section, compilers are expensive, and interpreters, which service scripted languages, are free.

One compromise that was decided upon was to incorporate the third-party search engine, Zoom, into Urantia Book Explorer. This was because no exemplar metric capability for a power search existed at that time and to embark upon pioneering the writing of search programs for *The Urantia Book*, would have meant a departure from the thrust of the development efforts.

Zoom's complexity and its ownership by a smaller company could adversely impact Urantia Book Explorer's maintenance and longevity, but this excellent package, used around the world, powerfully enabled Urantia Book readers to perform their searches.

Adding Multilinguality

The Multilingual Urantia Book project introduced the requirement, not present for Urantia Book Explorer, of *multilinguality*

Character encoding on the web up until then had normally

been accomplished on a given web page by invoking one of a range of sets of 256-characters each, a choice specified programmatically in terms of a particular ISO Standard, which had to be identified on the web page.

Unicode characters are specified by numbers. But ultimately, representing the unicode numbers in files requires a way of specifying those numbers with ones and zeros. a practice referred to as *character encoding*. Up until around that time, a common character encoding system for use with personal computers had been the standard called *ASCII* (American Standard Code for Information Exchange).

As a result of the Multilingual Urantia Book's newly appearing requirement for multilinguality, there simultaneously arose the requirement for a data processing programming language that had some way of handling all of the characters in all of the languages that might be involved. As a corollary, a requirement further existed for an application coding language that could handle all of the character sets (such a set is called a *script*) for all of those languages.

Unicode was selected to be the character encoding standard. The use of unicode for character encoding was a major step forward in the ability to manipulate characters in various languages simultaneously—and in the same document. But unicode was so new to technology — although it had already found its way into Microsoft software—that it was not yet incorporated in even the latest PHP interpreter, which had already been used heavily up to that point.

PERL for Windows—that is, *ActivePerl*—was chosen to replace PHP4 as the data processing programming language. PERL's then-latest release was the first scripting language, to my knowledge, to have any unicode capability.

There were certain problems with the PERL implementation of the unicode programming protocol, since unicode was new to the PERL interpreter, but they were not insurmountable.

A unicode file can be character-encoded in any of three different forms, or *transformations:*

1. 8-bit

2. 16-bit

3. 32-bit

4. UTF-8

The 8-bit version (which is actually a variable-width encoding) was chosen.

UTF-8 encoding is identical to ASCII encoding for the Latin character set (script), of which the English letters, numbers, and symbols are a subset, and grows to greater widths for other scripts.

Adding Language Neutrality

The primary task of the first, or data processing, phase of the Multilingual Urantia Book project was to reduce each of the 197 English language papers to the following two elements:

1. A set of 197 distilled plain text unicode files, each file corresponding to a separate paper in The Urantia Book. Each file would contain a separate record for each line of the encompassing paper. These files would contain no embellishment lines or blank lines.

2. A file whose contents comprise, by relative line number, a table of the attributes of each line in the text file (line type, etc).

This plan was carried out. The specific characteristics of every individual line in The Urantia Book were tabulated in machine form and became the basis and definition of Urantia Book Programming. The distilled Urantia Book text files are called *exemplar files* and retain italic and underline information and in-title line break information, as specified in a markdown language called the *Urantia Book Programming Language (UBPL)*. The table files are called *metrics files*.

Additional exemplar files were made for other language texts, which could then be manipulated in conjunction with the metrics files. One set of metrics files, unlike the exemplar files, is usable for all languages, because it contains information about the *organization* of the text, which does not change with language.

Thus was gained the ability for UBP to manipulate the text of all language versions of The Urantia Book without regard to the language involved, as long as exemplars for that language and the universal metrics for The Urantia Book were available.

Adding File Management

I recognized from the beginning that when the day should come to hand the Urantia Book programs over to some more permanent custodian than myself, there might be no IT professionals available who could maintain, upgrade, and operate them.

Because of this, and in recognition of problems that can be encountered with non-intuitive and abstract solutions, particularly where they involve a mapping, a departure from directly observed parameters, I decided to use flat files for all data and not to use any storage techniques involving mapping. Plain text files were to be the exclusive storage technique. (Unicode files, like ASCII files, though encoded, are still consideredk to be plain text files).

File naming would be of a specific design that would identify critical information about each file in its file name,
including the phase of the processing to which that file
might belong.

Adding File Handling

After completion of the Multilingual Urantia Book, the
Urantia Book Translator project brought the requirement
to read files from, and write files to, the respective client
computers.

Investigation turned up the existence of a type of web page
that can read and write files on client computers. Such
privileged web pages are in every sense real programs,
called *hypertext applications*, or *HTML applications*, each
identified and invoked by its filename, which has an extension of *.hta*. No special requirement exists for a file to be
qualified as a n HTML Application, except that it has to be
written in HTML and one or more scripting languages sup-
ported by Microsoft Internet Explorer, such as VBScript or
JavaScript.

It was decided to develop Urantia Book Translator as an
hta application.

Hta's typically use the *File System Object* to read and write
files. The File System Object cannot read or write UTF-8
files. But it can handle UTF-16LE files.

UTF-8 was already the unicode encoding method of the
Urantia Book Programming Protocol. A total of 19,730
Urantia Book files had already been processed and stored
in UTF-8. This included the 1,973 html files of the Multilingual Urantia Book (9 languages times 197 files for
each language), as well as these nine language's exemplar

files (called *normalized files* at that early time) in 9 stored phases of successive processing for each language.

(After Urantia Book Translator was subsequently completed, all 1,973 of the Multilingual Urantia Book's *html* files were then converted to UTF-16, as well as all 1,973 of the *exemplar* files for the nine languages.)

When coding was well under way, it was found that although PERL had properly written the unicode UTF-8 files previously for the Multilingual Urantia Book, it could not write UTF-16 files correctly. It failed to encode the CR and also the LF in 16 bits each, but encoded them instead in 8 bits each. This bug in the interpreter rendered PERL useless for developing Urantia Book Translator.

It was decided that, although later versions of PERL might become free of the CR-LF bug, the complexity of installing ActivePerl on PC's and the less than 100% rate of succes in installing ActivePerl on PC's disqualified PERL as a further programming language candidate for the Urantia Book Programming Paradigm.

Mapping The Urantia Book

Back near the completion of the Urantia Book Explorer project, I had created a paragraph map of the Uversa Press (Urantia Book Fellowship) 2003 edition using PHP to write and execute the mapping program. By this time, the mapping information was already available in distributed form in the totality of the descriptor record prefixes for each line in the normalized files.

The records in the early exemplar files, originally called normalized files, incorporated an individual descriptive prefix at the beginning of every line (record), which provided the textual reference descriptor for that line, in terms of the particular reference system for which he file was created. Information programmatically extracted from the complete set of prefixes for an entire Urantia Book and written as a single table file for the entire Urantia Book was the first Urantia Book metrics file. It was created for its designed central role in then-future Urantia Book data processing.

Soon after, with the beginning of the Multilingual Urantia Book project, PHP was again used to map the paragraphs in The Urantia Book, this time in terms of the Urantia Foundation's definition of paragraphs, not that of the Urantia Book Fellowship.

Standardizing Line Count

In the Urantia Book Translator Project, line-by-line correspondence across translations was extended to include the number of *sublines*, if any, in each section title line. The number of paragraph lines in each paper was easily kept constant across languages, also the number of lines in each paper title (always one line). But the number of lines in a certain few section titles was (understandably) found not to be constant across the eight non-english *translations* of The Urantia Book that had *already been created*.

Exactly fifteen section titles in the English first printing contain more than one line. These section titles appear in papers 42, 57, 59, 60, and 61. The number of lines in each section title was identified and recorded and a structural device was coded into Urantia Book Translator to ensure a fixed number of all lines, or records, in any given paper of *The Urantia Book* for all succeeding translations.

The 1,973 existing HTML files of the nine languages in The Multilingual Urantia Book and their corresponding 1,973 exemplar files were not back-checked for correctness of subline count in each section title. This remained to be done, and was never done in the fray of pressing new demands and relative priorities.

With the *line counts* thus held fixed and accounted for in the computer by a table of *section title subline counts*, the way was made clear for accurate, language-neutral data processing of the Urantia Book exemplar files to be accomplished through the use of the Urantia Book metrics files.

Expanding File Management

Upon completion of Urantia Book Translator, the project to develop Urantia Book Codifier was begun. Urantia Book Codifier was designed to manage the ongoing process of which Urantia Book Translator is only the data acquisition component, which provides sets of newly translated Urantia Book exemplar files for further processing and text manipulation. The large number of files normally processed in each step, the increasing number of language exemplar files and HTML files stored and accessed, and the increasing number of end-product and intermediate file types necessitated a central program like Urantia Book Codifier to computerize and simplify the expanding file management task.

Also, the potential for confusion engendered by large numbers of files in large numbers of stages in large numbers of languages, and by the dynamic and fast-moving nature of the process, necessitated some type of computer-discernible file-type and other-information designation on or in the files. An important UBPP protocol of having files contain only pure Urantia Book text ruled out any informational header records.

A file naming system was designed to make this information machine-discernible in the file names themselves. This also allowed for the clear visual human distinction between files containing the same data but in different stages of processing by inspecting their file names only.

All files in UTF-16LE format that are processed by the Urantia Book processing programs incorporate the extension, *.u16*, in their names unless they are required by the platform operating system to have another extension—for example, htm or html for web pages. In this case, they have the term, u16, in other, specified locations in the file name. These are all referred to as *u16 files*.

Urantia Book Codifier was put into operation at its completion, functioning as the conversion tool to interrelate the files going between various Urantia Book data processing programs or storage locations in the Urantia Book Data System by changing their names and, where required, their format, or even their contents. The programs thus coordinated by Urantia Book Codifier were themselves creating and/or modifying the files passing to them and from them.

The UBDS file naming protocol, in conjunction with Urantia Book Codifier, is what threads together the various programs and files involved in Urantia Book data processing into the Urantia Book Data System.

Metrics

About Metrics Files

Urantia Book metrics files are files that contain information about the organization—the structure—of *The Urantia Book*.

Metrics files that contain data about the English 1955 first printing are called *primary metrics files*, or *primary metrics*. All other metrics files, pertaining to various Urantia Book language editions—already in print or to be printed using them—are *secondary*. Metrics files are independent of the language of the textual content, except where *The Urantia Book* in a certain language has been designed to a language-specific book design that departs from the English and English-compliant formats.

Some metrics files contain a large number of data entries; for example, paragraph maps. Others can be short, as in the case of the metrics file containing the Paper Number:Section Number descriptors of the fifteen section titles in The Urantia Book that encompass multiple lines. Remember that it is only by adhering to line-by-line compliancy with the line formats of the first printing of theEnglish language Urantia Book that exemplar metrics, hence language neutrality, can work.

In the larger view, Urantia Book metrics files can be used for purposes ranging from converting Urantia Book text to various media—for example, creating web pages—to providing detailed attribute data for file analysis.

Fundamental Metrics Design

The *absolute*, or *abs,* paragraph reference system is used to identify individual paragraphs in *The Urantia Book* in terms of PaperNumber:SectionNumberInPaper.ParagraphNumberInSection, where paragraphs are recognized for definitional purposes by indentations in the English first printing and coded into computer files of all editions by delimiting them with CR-LF.

The primary advantage of the absolute paragraph reference system, as compared with other reference systems, is that it is self-defining and inherently machine-and-human recognizable.

Its self-definitional aspect is that it is defined directly in terms of the structure of The Urantia Book, with no introduced abstraction in terms of mapping.

Its inherent *human-recognition* aspect is that the system

is linear: once the designation rule is learned, a human can work out the designation for any given paragraph by observing the location of the paragraph in the organizational framework of *The Urantia Book*. Its inherent *machine-recognition* aspect is the same as that for human recognition coupled with the fact that each paragraph, defined to humans by indentation, is simultaneously defined to computers through its delimiting with CRLF, which computers can sense.

The design goal for those Urantia Book metrics that involve large numbers of data points—for example, a table that specifies individual attributes of each paragraph in the Urantia Book—is to design innovative data structures tailored, for each instance, to hold maximum information in minimum data entries. This can involve designing the data so that moderate calculation is required at processing time to obtain certain quantities.

Consider the following array of seven numbers:

3, 12, 15, 5, 7, 17, 9

This one-dimensional array happens to be the absolute paragraph map for Paper 3 of The Urantia Book. It holds more information than might at first be apparent.

Explicitly, this array identifies the number of paragraphs in each section of Paper 3.

But *non-explicitly*, it also gives the number of sections in the paper. The number of sections in Paper 3 can be obtained from the above array through calculation. Since each element in the array gives the number of paragraphs in a single section, in increasing order, in the paper, then the number of sections in Paper 3 is equal to the array length; that is, to the number of elements in the array. This metric for Paper 3 is made up of 7 numbers, or elements.

Thus, Paper 3 has 7 sections. This is true no matter what the language.

In terms of the organization of The Urantia Book, the section number of the section to which each paragraph count applies in this array is also discernible, but not explicitly. The section in Paper 3 that contains 5 paragraphs, for example, is seen to be the fourth section in the paper, which is Section 3 (the first section is always Section 0).

More information, yet, is available from the above paragraph map. The total number of lines in the paper is also non-explicitly available. Examining the array and visualizing the paper in terms of the logic that one would code into the computer to carry out this task, the paper is seen to be made up of one title line for the paper title, plus one title line for every section except the first, plus the sum of all the section sizes.

Thus, from the array above, Paper 3 has $1 + 6 + 68 = 75$ lines. (All multiline section titles have been normalized to occupy only one line in storage). And the number of exemplar records in the exemplar file for Paper 3, regardless of the language involved, is 75, 1 exemplar record for each line of text in Paper 3.

The information accessible from this simple, one-dimensional array is still not exhausted. Imagine that a program processing an exemplar file containing the text of Paper 3 needed to identify the line type of every line, or record, in the file as it is read, in order to format each line for a web page or a print file, or maybe to compile some statistics or carry out an analysis.

It is clear from the paragraph map that line 1 of the file would be the paper title, then the three paragraphs comprising Section 0 would be encountered, then the section title line of Section 1, followed by the the 12 lines of Section 1, each of which would be a paragraph line. The line identification process is easily carried out through the processing of the entire file of Paper 3.

Shown below is the first part of the absolute paragraph map file for the entire Urantia Book in terms of its 197 papers, designed to contain its information in such compact form that it can be listed in just 197 lines. For easy incorporation as an *include file* (separate files that are processed as being part of the program code) in various UBP programs, this information is stored in the include file formatted as the code defining a two-dimensional JavaScript array literal, which is already filled with its values.

Each line of the absolute Urantia Book paragraph map is an element of the outer array and is itself a single one-dimensional array of numbers constituting the paragraph map of one Urantia Book paper. The fourth line, below, is outer element element 3 of the Urantia Book abs paragraph map. Its set of numbers is therefore the paragraph map for Paper 3.

By this means, the structural characteristics of the entire Urantia Book are stored in the space of just 197 lines.

```
//-----------------------------------
var absMapArray =
[
/* Paper0 */  [6, 26, 18, 25, 13, 12, 13, 10, 12, 5, 2, 16, 13],
/* paper1 */  [6, 6, 10, 8, 7, 16, 8, 9],
/* Paper2 */  [3, 11, 7, 6, 5, 12, 9, 13],
/* Paper3 */  [3, 12, 15, 5, 7, 17, 9],
/* Paper4 */  [3, 12, 8, 7, 9, 8],
/* Paper5 */  [2, 12, 6, 8, 15, 14, 14],
/* (etc.) */
```

//-------------------------------------

Coded Metrics Design

The *Urantia Foundation*, or *ufn*, paragraph reference system is another system used to identify individual paragraphs in *The Urantia Book*, but in the format of *PageNumberInBook.ParagraphNumberOnPage*.

The problem with the ufn system is that the quantities it involves fail to reference *The Urantia Book*'s *organizational* structure, based on its *content*. Instead, they reference its *physical* structure, based on its *pagination*. Thus, the ufn system is only valid for specific editions of *The Urantia Book*, and only for specific media presentations.

In the ufn reference system, broken paragraphs at the top of a page—that is, paragraphs that begin on the previous page and continue to the current page, are given the number 0. Intact, non-broken paragraphs at the top of a page are given the number 1.

Therefore, the basis of the numbering of paragraphs on pages is variable, depending on whether the first paragraph on the page is or is not broken.

In addition, broken paragraphs at the bottom of a page—that is, paragraphs that begin on the current page and continue to the next page, are given the number corresponding to their relative paragraph on the current page, in either a zero- or 1-based count, depending on the completeness of the top paragraph on the current page.

Shown below is the first part of the Urantia Foundation paragraph map file for the entire Urantia Book in terms of its 2,097 pages, designed to contain its information in such compact form that it can be listed in just 210 lines.

//-------------------------------------

```
var ufnParagraphMapArray = [0,
/*1*/  6, -14, 19, -14, 19, -8, 11, 10, -11, 11,
/*11*/  -14, -6, 7, -9, 9, -8, 3, 0, 0, 0,
/*21*/  3, 6, -6, -9, 6, 7, -6, -8, 7, 7,
/*31*/  8, -2, 4, -7, -7, -8, -5, -7, -8, -7,
/*41*/  6, 8, -7, 5, -7, 6, 6, -9, -7, -7,
/*51*/  13, 5, -8, 5, 6, 7, -8, 9, -7, -7,
//------------------------------------
```

Each line in the above table listing contains metrics for 10 Urantia Book pages (Urantia Foundation editions only), and is an array of 10 numbers, each number specifying the number of complete or partial paragraphs on the corresponding page in ascending sequence of page number. Thus, on line 1 of data, the third number, which is 19, specifies that page 3 of The Urantia Book (ufn) contains 19 paragraphs, as paragraphs are defined in the ufn paragraph reference system.

Since the entity that contains these counts—that is, a page—does not necessarily begin or end with a complete paragraph, the idea of a *count of paragraphs* on a page is meaningless (in the integral sense), and the number shown is currently used only to specify the sometimes mixed number of full and partial paragraphs on the page: i.e., first page (full and partial) paragraphs, second page (full and partial) paragraphs, and so on up to the the number of pages listed in the table.

So that it can be determined, for a given page, whether to refer to that page's first paragraph as paragraph 0 or paragraph 1, the table must also specify, for each page, whether the first paragraph on that page is broken or unbroken. The last paragraph on the page can also be broken, but its broken/non-broken status does not affect its relative sequence number on the page, hence the sequential count of paragraphs on the page, as shown in the table.

The vagaries of the ufn paragraph reference system resulted in the introduction into Urantia Book metrics of the practice of *coding*, or *mapping*, certain information. Rather than record a second attribute in the ufn paragraph map for every individual page in The Urantia Book, the metric design for this map specifies that positive numbers shall signify a page beginning with an unbroken first paragraph and negative numbers shall signify a broken first paragraph for the page. The *magnitude* of the number in both cases remains unchanged: in the listing above, the final two values for line 1 specify that page 9 contains 11 paragraphs (-11) and begins with a broken paragraph, while page 10 also contains 11 paragraphs but begins with an unbroken paragraph (11).

Computer functions that need information from the ufn paragraph map can determine the number of paragraphs beginning (but not necessarily ending) on a page by using the absolute value stored as the argument of the page number (the JavaScript abs() function). The value 0 or 1, which would represent a broken or unbroken first paragraph, respectively, could easily be obtained for the first paragraph by a conditional logic statement, such as

firstNumber = paraMap[pageNumber] > 0 ? 1 : 0;

Since the idea of the number of paragraphs on a page has no meaning, neither does the idea of the number of paragraphs in a range of pages.

The Second Society Foundation, or ***ssf***, reference system is based on the format of Urantia Book citations in the work, *A Study of The Master Universe*, by William S. Sadler Jr., published by the Second Society Foundation in 1968. Most in-depth secondary works written before the publication of the Uversa Press Edition used the ssf reference system for citing Urantia Book text, though this system was not given a name, since no other reference system had then been used, except the system used by Clyde Bedell in the *Concordex of The Urantia Book*, which specified location on the page in terms of the vertical quartering of each page into parts A, B, C, and D.

The ssf system is identical to the ufn system, which was defined later than the ssf system, with the exception that in the ssf system, the first paragraph on each page is always given the number, 1, whether it is a complete paragraph or a broken paragraph.

The ssf paragraph designations can also be determined from the ufn paragraph map, by using the absolute values of the arguments to obtain paragraph counts on the page regardless of broken/unbroken status, and always giving the first paragraph or portion of a paragraph on a page the number, 1. The same problem with summing the number of paragraphs exists in the ssf reference system as in the ufn reference system.

Custom Metrics Design

In addition to the absolute paragraph reference system, based entirely on inherently machine detectable text units that are defined in terms of the organization of the textual content of The Urantia Book, and the ufn and the ssf paragraph reference systems, based on a combination of inherently machine detectable text units (paragraphs) that are defined in terms of the organization of the textual content of The Urantia Book and not-inherently-machine-detectable text units (pages) that are not defined in terms of the organization of the textual content of The Urantia Book, there is a possibility of other relevant paragraph reference systems.

For example, the Uversa Press (Urantia Book Fellowship),

or *ubf*, paragraph reference system, like the absolute paragraph reference system, is based on PaperNumberInBook, SectionNumberInPaper, and also ParagraphNumberInSection. However, it defines paragraphs differently than does the abs system. In the ubf system, a paragraph can be—as defined by the Urantia Book Fellowship on a case-by-case basis—either a single *paragraph* or a single *cluster of contiguous paragraphs* as paragraphs are defined in the abs system.

A ubf paragraph map, then, would have to include all the types of information that are included in an abs paragraph map, and in addition, show where paragraph clustering does and does not occur. It would further have to show, for each composite paragraph, composed of a cluster of non-clustered, or elementary, paragraphs, how many elementary paragraphs make up that composite paragraph and identify which specific elementary paragraphs are in which composite paragraphs.

Shown below is the first part of the Urantia Book Fellowship, or ubf, paragraph map file for the entire Urantia Book in terms of its 197 papers, designed to contain its information in such compact form that it can be listed in just 197 lines.

```
//-------------------------------------
var ubfConstructor =
[
/* Paper 0 */  [[6], [18, -8], [1, -4, 13], [-8, 17], [13],
[12], [13], [1, -3, 6], [-8, 4], [5], [2], [16], [13]],
/* Paper 1 */  [[6], [6], [2, -4, 4], [8], [7], [16], [8], [9]],
/* Paper 2 */  [[3], [11], [7], [6], [5], [12], [9], [13]],
/* Paper 3 */  [[3], [12], [10, -4, 1], [5], [7], [17], [9]],
/* Paper 4 */  [[3], [12], [8], [7], [9], [8]],
/* Paper 5 */  [[2], [12], [6], [8], [9, -4, 2], [14], [14]],
```

The ubf paragraph map is a three-dimensional array. The outer index is the paper number, the middle index is the section number, and the inner index is the count of paragraphs in the section.

Notice that on a given line, which is the portion of the map pertaining to a specific paper, most of the numbers are single-element arrays. The reason for having arrays of only one element is for logical and iterative purposes, giving the paragraph map the ability to be accessed completely by three-dimensional iteration based on the machine-detectable length of every outer and middle element in the array. Single-element arrays, under this technique, are iterated from a low index value of 1 to a high index value of 1. In lines (papers) where all the numbers are single-element arrays, the numbers are identical to those of the abs paragraph map array—for example in line 3 (Paper 2) above.

Where the paragraph count in a section involves both unclustered paragraphs and clustered paragraphs, the innermost array, representing the paragraphs in that section, must include separate counts of the clustered and unclustered paragraphs, at the same time making the specific location and identity of the elementary paragraphs comprising the clustered paragraphs clear, and making the location of the clustered paragraphs, within the section, clear.

This is accomplished within the innermost arrays by signifying the run sizes of unclustered paragraphs and the cluster sizes of clustered paragraphs separately by positive and negative numbers, respectively, the magnitudes of these numbers specifying the number of paragraphs in the run or cluster, as the case may be.

The partial ubf paragraph map above specifies that Paper

3 has seven sections (the number of inner arrays). That six of these sections are composed solely of unclustered paragraphs (since six sections are single element arrays having a positive number for their single elements). The remaining section, Section 2, represented by the third inner array, is composed of ten unclustered paragraphs (positive number, 10) followed by a single clustered paragraph composed of four elementary paragraphs (paragraphs 11 through14), which is finally followed by one elementary paragraph.

By accessing the abs, the ufn, or the ubf paragraph map, a Urantia Book program could gain heretofore unimaginable power to convert the text of The Urantia Book, in any translated language, from the exemplar text files into various formats for various purposes. Analyses could be performed. Integrity checks could be carried out.

An approximate check for italics correspondence across languages, for example, has already been designed conceptually but not scheduled for development. Further metrics files could be created to show relationships between parameters explicitly or implicitly contained in the abs, ufn, and ubf paragraph maps. Paragraph maps for new reference systems could be created. Metrics files could be made to direct the conversion of The Urantia Book into yet further forms and formats.

The existing paragraph maps could be used in new ways to solve seemingly unsolvable current problems; for example, the problem of specifying, by computer means, the handling of lists in the text.

As an example, the exemplar files could produce Urantia Books that would automatically be marked with paragraph designations of the absolute reference system, being instructed to suppress the marking of paragraphs that in the ubf paragraph map are seen to be elementary components of clustered paragraphs, and to set off the beginnings and endings of such clustered paragraphs, or lists, with a preceding and succeeding blank line.

Other paragraphs in the text of The Urantia Book could be identified, from examining the English first printing, as good places to precede or succeed with a blank line, and corresponding metrics files could be created.

This would be done without affecting the exemplar files, which, under the UBP Protocol, remain unvarying, containing no formatting lines.

Exemplars

About Exemplar Files

In exemplar files, each file contains the distilled text of one Urantia Book paper. Each record contains one one line of distilled text preceded by a square-bracketed number then a single space, the number showing the position of the line in the Urantia Book. Records are in ascending order on sequence number and are each terminated by a CRLF.

The first portions of the exemplar files for Paper 1 in four languages are shown as examples below, dramatically illustrating the power of the language-neutral line-by-line correspondence of the text of *The Urantia Book* made possible by the use of exemplars.

English -Paper 1 (Lines 1-4)

[1] PAPER 1. THE UNIVERSAL FATHER

[2] THE Universal Father is the God of all creation, the First Source and Center of all things and beings. First think of God as a creator, then as a controller, and lastly as an infinite upholder. The truth about the Universal Father had

begun to dawn upon mankind when the prophet said: "You, God, are alone; there is none beside you. You have created the heaven and the heaven of heavens, with all their hosts; you preserve and control them. By the Sons of God were the universes made. The Creator covers himself with light as with a garment and stretches out the heavens as a curtain." Only the concept of the Universal Father—one God in the place of many gods—enabled mortal man to comprehend the Father as divine creator and infinite controller.

[3] The myriads of planetary systems were all made to be eventually inhabited by many different types of intelligent creatures, beings who could know God, receive the divine affection, and love him in return. The universe of universes is the work of God and the dwelling place of his diverse creatures. "God created the heavens and formed the earth; he established the universe and created this world not in vain; he formed it to be inhabited."

[4] The enlightened worlds all recognize and worship the Universal Father, the eternal maker and infinite upholder of all creation. The will creatures of universe upon universe have embarked upon the long, long Paradise journey, the fascinating struggle of the eternal adventure of attaining God the Father. The transcendent goal of the children of time is to find the eternal God, to comprehend the divine nature, to recognize the Universal Father. God-knowing creatures have only one supreme ambition, just one consuming desire, and that is to become, as they are in their spheres, like him as he is in his Paradise perfection of personality and in his universal sphere of righteous supremacy. From the Universal Father who inhabits eternity there has gone forth the supreme mandate, "Be you perfect, even as I am perfect." In love and mercy the messengers of Paradise have carried this divine exhortation down through the ages and out through the universes, even to such lowly animal-origin creatures as the human races of Urantia.

Russian - Paper 1 (Lines 1-4)

[1] ДОКУМЕНТ 1. ОТЕЦ ВСЕГО СУЩЕГО

[2] ВСЕОБЩИЙ Отец является Богом всего творения, Первым Источником и Центром всех вещей и существ. Думайте о Боге прежде всего как о создателе, затем как о властителе и только потом — как о бесконечном вседержителе. Истина о Всеобщем Отце стала открываться человечеству со словами пророка: «Един ты, Боже, и нет иного. Тобою сотворены небеса и небеса небес и всё их воинство; ты хранишь их и властвуешь над ними. Сынами Божьими были созданы вселенные. Творец одевается светом, словно ризой, простирает небеса, словно ткань». Только представление о Всеобщем Отце — едином Боге вместо многих — позволило смертному человеку осмыслить Отца как божественного создателя и бесконечного властителя.

[3] Мириады планетарных систем сотворены для того, чтобы со временем здесь могли поселиться различные типы разумных созданий, — существ, которые способны познать Бога, принять божественную любовь и полюбить его в ответ. Вселенная вселенных является Божьим творением и местом обитания его разнообразных созданий. «Бог сотворил небеса и образовал землю; не напрасно он утвердил вселенную и создал этот мир; он образовал его для жительства».

[4] Все просвещенные миры признат Всеобщего Отца и поклоняются ему — вечному творцу и бесконечному вседержителю всего творения. Волевые создания великого множества вселенных вступили на долгий, долгий путь к Раю — увлекательное преодоление трудностей, сопровождающее вечное путешествие, обретение Бога-Отца. Трансцендентальная цель детей времени — найти вечного Бога, осмыслить

его божественную сущность, узнать Всеобщего Отца. Богопознавшие создания охвачены только одним высочайшим стремлением, только одной всепоглощающей страстью: начав свой путь такими, какими они являются в своих сферах, стать подобными ему, Райскому совершенству его личности во всеобщей сфере праведного господства. Высочайший наказ обитающего в вечности Всеобщего Отца гласит: «Будьте совершенны, как совершенен я». С любовью и милосердием пронесли посланники Рая эту божественную проповедь сквозь века и вселенные, придя с нею и к таким скромным созданиям животного происхождения, как человеческий род Урантии.

Korean - Paper 1 (Lines 1-4)

[1] 제 1 편. 우주 아버지

[2] 우주 아버지는 모든 창조의 하느님이시며, 모든 사물과 존재의 첫째근원이며 중심이다. 우선 하느님을 창조자로서, 다음에는 조정자로서, 그리고 맨 나중에는 무한한 유지자로서 생각하라. 예언자들이 "하느님, 당신은 홀로 계시며 ; 당신 외에는 아무도 없습니다. 당신은 하늘을 창조하셨고 또한 하늘들의 하늘을 그곳의 모든 무리들과 함께 창조하셨으며 ; 이들을 보존하고 조정하십니다. 우주들은 하느님의 아들들에 의하여 만들어졌습니다. 창조주는 빛으로 옷처럼 자신을 두루고 있으며 휘장처럼 하늘들을 펼치십니다."라고 말했을 때에 우주 아버지에 대한 진리가 인류에게 밝혀지기 시작하였다. 오직 우주 아버지의 개념 ― 많은 하느님들 대신 한 하느님 ― 만이 필사사람으로 하여금 아버지를 신성한 창조자와 무한한 조정자로서 이해할 수 있게 하였다.

[3] 무수한 행성 체계들은 모두 결국에는 여러 종류의 많은 지능(知能)창조체들, 하느님을 알 수 있고, 신성한 애정을 받아들이고, 보답으로 그를 사랑할 수 있

는 존재들이 거주되도록 만들어졌다. 우주들의 우주는 하느님의 작품이며 그의 다양한 창조체들이 사는 곳이다. "하느님이 하늘들을 창조하셨고 땅을 빚으셨으며; 하느님이 우주를 세우셨고 이 세상을 헛되이 창조하지 않으셨으며; 거주되도록 그것을 빚으셨다."

[4] 깨우친 세계들 모두는 모든 창조의 영원한 조물주이며 무한의 유지자인 우주 아버지를 인식하고 그리고 경배한다. 우주 위의 우주마다 모든 의지 창조체들은 길고 긴 낙원천국으로의 여행, 아버지 하느님께 도달하는 영원한 모험인 황홀한 투쟁을 시작했다. 시간의 자녀들의 초월적 목표는 영원한 하느님을 발견하는 것, 신성한 본성을 이해하는 것, 우주 아버지를 인식하는 것이다. 하느님을-아는 창조체들은 오직 한 가지 최극의 열망, 온몸을 불태우는 욕망 하나를 갖고 있으니, 이는 그들이 그들의 구체들에 있어서도, 그가 그의 개인성의 낙원천국 완전성으로 그리고 그의 의로운 최극위(最極位)의 우주 구체에서 존재하는 그러한 그 같이 되어가는 것이다. 영원에 거하는 우주 아버지로부터 최극의 명령이 내려졌다, "내가 완전한 것처럼 너희들도 완전하라." 낙원천국의 사자(使者)들은 사랑과 자비로써 이 간곡하고도 신성한 권유를 여러 세대에 걸쳐 아래쪽으로 그리고 여러 우주를 거쳐 바깥쪽으로, 심지어는 유란시아의 인종들과 같은 하등의 동물-기원 창조체에게까지 전해 왔다.

Arabic - Paper 1 (Lines 1-4)

[1] المقالة 1. الآب الشامل

[2] الآب الشامل هو الله كل الخلق, المصدر والمركز الأول لكل الأشياء والكائنات. أولاً فـّكر عن الله كخالق, ثم كمتحكم, وأخيراً كداعم لانهائي. ابتدأت الحقيقة عن الله الشامل بالبزوغ على جنس الإنسان عندما قال النبي: "أنت الله وحدك, لا يوجد أحد سواك. أنت خلقت السماء وسماء السماوات وكل جماهيرها؛ تحفظهم وتتحكم بهم. بأبناء

الله صُنعت الأكوان. يغطي الخالق ذات بنور كما موهفملا طقف "راتستك تاوامسلا طسببيو عادرب برد عع الآل بآ لماشلا ــ هللا دحاو نكامن ةدع ةلآ ــ هَلَإ يرشبلا ناسنإلا رّدق ليفهم الآب الخالق إلى .يئانانلا مكحتم وهمحتم

[3] اهلك تلعجُ ىصص حـَت لا يتلا ةيبكوكلا ةمظنألا ةفلتخمل لكاشألاب ةنوكسم ةجيتنلا نوكت يف لتكنوت ةريثك نم تاقولخملا ,ةيكذلا تائنكاتن ردقت معرفة من ,اللّه عطفت الإلهيّة, وتحجب في هله سكن ومركز هللا لمع وه ناوكألا نوك .لباقملاب سَسَأو تاوامسلا هللا قلخ "خلق. هتاقولخم ةعونتم أثبع لَمالعلا اذه قلخيو نوكلا سسؤي مل ؛ضرألا لنصنع مسكناً."انوكسم نوكيل

[4] لك ملاوعلا متنورةتعترف بآلاب لماشلا لكل يئاهانلاللا مادلاو يدبألا لماعلا ,هدبعتو قوف ناوكأ يف ةئيشملا تاقولخملا ترشاب .قلخلا ,سودرفلل ةليوطلا ةلحرلا ىلع ناوكأ أ هللا زارحإل ةيدبألا ةرماغملا يف نتافاصرلا راعلصرا داجيإل وه ناو نمزلا ءانبأ لأبنان دهف يلاعتملا .الآب فرعتلل ,ةيهَلإلا ةعيبطلا مهفلو يدبألا هللا هللا ةفراعلا تاقولخملا لماشلا بآلا ىلع ةلغاشلاعلى دحاو ةبغر ,طقف حموم ساسي طيادلاها لثم ,اهئاوجأ يف ىه امك ريصتلا لكتلو ,طقف يفو ةيصخش نم يسودرفلا هلامك يف وه امك يذلا لماشلا بآلا نم .راب ومس نم لماشلا هوج ةيماسلا ةيروموأملا تقلطناةدبألا نكسي ةبحم يف "يكامك انأ امك ىتح ,نيييلاماك اونوك" رورحم,حمل رلاسالنين نم سودرفلا هذه ةصصيح ,ةيهَلإلا نزولا لالخ جاراخو رصصور علا جارَ لالا الألا ناوكأ يناويح لصأ نم ةعيضولو تاقولخملا ىلإ ىتح لثم ةيناسنإلا ناسنإلا ةيناسورورليل اياشن.

3

Functions

Concepts

Text Access Method

Input data in Urantia Book Programming is usually a combination of two types: text and metrics. Both are stored in sequential access method, as plain text flat files.

The Urantia Book Programming approach is to convert these data at run time to direct access method for maximum speed. This access method conversion is carried out by a cyclic method of phased conversion, as will be explained.

In a batch operation, the exemplar files are read in and processed as individual files; that is, the processing is carried out in 197 iterations, one for each Urantia Book paper, thus inputting the entire text of The Urantia Book. Each paper is read into an array in memory, where it remains as that paper is processed. The inputting of each file is done as fast as possible: for example,

- record-by-record for some programs, where record screening or conversion is necessary, or

- full-file gulp in other programs, where no input processing is necessary, followed by a split() call to convert the aggregate text screen into an array of the plain text exemplars.

Thus, an overhead time-price is paid in one-time *reading and initializing* of the records in each file (as required) during the iteration cycle when that file is to be processed, but the *full speed of direct access* is subsequently available during the *entire processing* of that file. The index position of each input text record in the *text array* holding the entire paper identifies each individual input record in terms of line number (record number) within paper, which will serve as a lookup key in inputted *metrics arrays* to retrieve attributes of the individual text lines of the paper.

Similarly, text output files can either be: 1) written record-by-record from the text array, through iteration, or 2) accumulated in a single expanding string of iteratively calculated and concatenated CR-delimited substrings of, for example, HTML output, then written after completion of the entire iterative process as a whole file.

Output exemplar text files are written iteratively but individually, 197 files, one at a time, in the orderly flow of overall program iteration.

Metrics Access Method

Urantia Book metrics files, which are constantly referred to during a processing run that employs them, are specifically designed to contain a maximum of information in a minimum of space. This allows the loading and use of entire sets of metrics files, each set pertaining to *the entire Urantia Book* rather than only to *individual papers*, thereby endowing UBP programs with fast and easy access to metrics data, free from the file management complications that would accompany paper-by-paper metrics file storage.

For maximum speed, a metrics file that is to be used in a processing run is stored in memory as an array, which may be a one-, two-, or three-dimensional array, depending on the particular metrics. For ease of access, the metrics files are already stored in files as JavaScript arrays, to be used as include files in the code of the programs that use them, thereby becoming accessible by direct access method in memory at program startup.

Iterative Precalculation and Metrics Expansion

During processing for a given Urantia Book paper, whose text lines are all going to be stored and processed as separate array elements in memory, it is productive of speed, efficiency, and more direct iterative coding to:

1. Precalculate, and store in memory as arrays, text-line-specific derivative metrics that are implicit, but not explicit, in the full Urantia Book-length metrics stored in arrays in memory, and

2. Apply these metrics and other calculated attributes to the text lines that are stored in arrays in memory.

   Instead of carrying out these two types of activity separately as each text line is being processed, two types of arrays are created and populated before the loading of each text file.

   First, before each paper is loaded, elements are accessed from the portion of the Urantia Book-length metrics file array in memory that contains metrics for the particular paper to be loaded, and derivative metrics are calculated from these and stored in a paper-wide metrics array.

   Second, as guided by the metrics in the paper-wide metrics array, an array is created in memory with exactly enough elements to hold all the text lines of the paper that is to be loaded. Then each element of this array is fashioned into an object with properties calculated for the text line that will be associated with that element and stored as attribute data in that object (using dot notation).

This is in anticipation of the actual loading of the paper and storing of the text lines in the array. The subsequent text lines, when they are loaded, are then stored in the appropriate array elements in the form of further object properties. Iterative processing then proceeds for the entire paper's elements using the information thus calculated and made directly accessible in memory.

Techniques

DOM Text Manipulation and Retrieval

A *Document Object Model (DOM)* is an *API (Application Programming Interface)* that defines a tree structure of *events, methods, objects, and properties* provided by a specific application to programs choosing it as their host platform. Microsoft's Internet Explorer DOM played a large role in Urantia Book Programming. Urantia Book Programming programs are written in an HTML framework and originally made use only of the Internet Explorer services, later cross-platforming their reach to include the Google Chrome web browser, as well.

In addition to manipulating the display of text, the DOM is variously used in UBP programs to create *WYSIWYG (what you see is what you get)*, HTML-based text editing capabilities and also to retrieve edited and calculated data and text for writing to files. Urantia Book Translator, for example, carries out text editing by means of DOM-facilitated HTML based manual editing of the text of The Urantia Book, in various languages.

Using Microsoft's Internet Explorer has its advantages and its disadvantages.

I was brought to it by its then almost 100% world market share and, further encouraged by the outstanding collection of important services of its DOM, which were missing from all other web browsers, I enthusiastically chose it to be UBP's host browser.

There were dangers, though, to using Internet Explorer's DOM. Other browsers adhered pretty much to the world standards, as they provided a common, but primitive, collection of services. But Microsoft showed its chosen path early by ignoring world standards, thereby being free to offer a more powerful collection of services *to those using its browser*.

This Put Microsoft in the driver's seat in being able subsequently to unilaterally change its Internet Explorer services, in which case all programs using them were forced to rewrite their code. Also, persons and groups who had time invested in code for the IE DOM were already committed to it in various ways; for example, in training and documentation.

Further, there was a *hidden* danger of using Internet Explorer's DOM, which was not bound by regulation from anyone but Microsoft. I became aware of this hidden danger when programs and routines of mine that had been working satisfactorily started to misbehave.

Troubleshooting these problems, I discovered some *transformations of my data* that were *undocumented by Microsoft*. Since Microsoft was not a party to the world standards for DOM's, it was their prerogative to do this.

I found that the IE DOM *actually altered my HTML coding*. For example, during troubleshooting, I programmatically wrote HTML to the *innerHTML* property of a

```
<div>
```

element. The HTML I wrote contained italics marked with

<i> </i>

tag pairs. When I then retrieved the innerHTML text string that I had written, it had been *unexplainably altered* by Internet Explorer to read, instead,

<em> </em>

Although this does not change the way the marked-up text is rendered (though it may someday, if Microsoft changes their tag definitions), it did create errors in the execution of some of my UBP JavaScript functions,

For example, in a UBP routine that I used to convert HTML to UBPL (Urantia Book Programming Language), which is a markdown language that I developed to preserve essential formatting as it was used in the English first printing ofThe Urantia Book). I had previously, for some time, followed the practice of accessing the innerHTML code of the text to be converted and then searching the retrieved innerHTML strings for the tag pair

<i> </i>,

next changing the tag pair to

{i{i{ }i}i,

which specifies italics in the UBPL language.

Full days can be spent tracking down the source of problems like these. Even though after they have been discovered, I can solve them, through *reactive coding*, still, undocumented *remappings might be introduced* by the browser maker, *time after time*, injecting mysterious problems into already tested and operating UBP programs.

DOM Text Location and Placement

In The Multilingual Urantia Book, each of the two paragraphs in the side-by-side bilingual display is a DOM element. For each corresponding text couplet sharing the same SRT numbers, the program computes screen coordinates, based on the calculated height of the tallest of the two preceding corresponding paragraphs and their topmost starting points, the point at which to align the tops of the couplet. These two paragraphs are then each independently positioned to the calculated positions.

In Urantia Book Translator, which was developed later, side-by-side paragraph placement was handled in a much simpler way; namely, by placing both paragraphs in a shared common container extending the breadth of the two combined, which was then positioned vertically, with the two automatically being positioned as well.

Using the DOM as a virtual *array of pointers* to text elements as they are stored in DOM elements is a useful innovation. Especially where, as for example in the *Translator's Dictionary* editing process in Urantia Book Translator, new words must be added at the correct alphabetical positions in a list, and edited words must be deleted from the list and re-inserted at the correct alphabetical location. This is carried out by a speedy function that applies a binary sort to an array of pointers to DOM objects using the innerText property of the objects, after copying the innerText property and mapping the copy to all-lower-case for the sort (to avoid case-sensitive sorting).

In Urantia Book Translator, the saving of the file in the Translator's Dictionary editing process was accomplished by maintaining an array of plain text words that were a mirror image of the words in the DOM elements, as editing goes on, and saving the text from this array. The binary sort for injecting elements into the proper location was also carried out on the plain text array mirror, which was then copied in its entirety to the array of innerText properties.

In Urantia Book Codifier, the *save* process was improved by saving directly from the individual innerText properties of the DOM itself, negating the need for a mirror array of text and the full array copying back and forth. The binary sort was also applied directly to the DOM's innerText properties. This improvement is envisioned for retrofitting into Urantia Book Translator, as well.

Innovation for Efficiency

One functional innovation in Urantia Book programming is to add leading zeros to string numerics by means of array index selection rather than by conditional logic. This is done in the zeroedPaperNumber (paperNumber) function, which converts numeric strings into 3-digit, leading-zero numeric strings. The function accomplishes this by the following code, which obtains the correct-length zero-fill string from a small array by using 3 minus the length of the numeric string to be modified as the array index:

```
//------------------------------------
// function zeroedPaperNumber (paperNumber)
//------------------------------------
function zeroedPaperNumber (paperNumber)
 {
 var stringPaperNumber = String(paperNumber);
 var stringPaperNumberLength = stringPaperNumber.length;
 if (stringPaperNumber.length < 3)
  {
  var zeros = ["", "0", "00"];
  var numberOfZerosToInsert = 3 - stringPaperNumberLength;
  var theZeroedPaperNumber = zeros[numberOfZerosToInsert] + stringPaperNumber;
  }
```

```
else
{
  var theZeroedPaperNumber = stringPaperNum-
ber;
}
return theZeroedPaperNumber;
}
```

Metrics Expansion and Precalculation

In the iterative processing of each paper as a processing unit, in anticipation of all the lines of the next paper being loaded into an array for processing, corresponding metrics information is precalculated and loaded into arrays for efficiency in the processing of the lines, which will then follow.

For example, in Urantia Book Codifier, when the full set of text lines of a Urantia Book paper is being processed in a run that is to produce output labeled in the absolute paragraph reference system, the

```
absIdentifier (absLineNumberInPaper)
```

function provides each line in turn with its individual paragraph identifier by a single line of code, as follows:

```
//------------------------------------
// function absIdentifier (absLineNumberInPaper)
//------------------------------------
function absIdentifier (absLineNumberInPaper)
{
  return absLineIdentifierArray[absLineNumberIn-
Paper];
}
```

The function simply returns a single element in an array of absolute line identifiers that is already filled and waiting.

In anticipation of their being needed, these line identifiers are precalculated and loaded into an array of all the identifiers for a given paper just before that paper is to be processed and the lines of that paper are loaded into an array of text lines.

If the paragraph designations are to be in the absolute paragraph reference system, the following function calculates all of the identifiers, based on the properties of the lines of text that will be loaded, as these properties are explicitly or implicitly recorded in the abs paragraph map. The function loads these calculated paragraph designations into an array at index values corresponding to the lineNumber-InPaper of text that they were respectively calculated for. The code of this expansion and precalculation function, fillAbsLineIdentifierArray (paperNumber), follows (refer to previous discussions and listing of abs paragraph map):

```
//-----------------------------------
// function fillAbsLineIdentifierArray (paperNum-
ber)
//-----------------------------------
function fillAbsLineIdentifierArray (paperNumber)
  {
  absLineIdentifierArray = [];
  numberOfLinesInPaper = 0;
  sectionNumberInPaper = 0;
  paragraphNumberInSection = 0;
  var lineIndex = 0;
  var lineNumberInPaper = 0;
  absLineIdentifierArray[0] = "0.0.0";
  for (var sectionIndex = 0; sectionIndex < absMap-
Array[paperNumber].length; sectionIndex++)
    {
    for (paragraphIndex = 0; paragraphIndex <
```

```
absMapArray[paperNumber][sectionIndex] + 1;
paragraphIndex++)

    {
    if (paperNumber != 139 || sectionIndex != 10)
    {
    absLineIdentifierArray[lineNumberInPaper]
= paperNumber + "." + sectionIndex + "." + para-
graphIndex;
    lineNumberInPaper++;
    }
    }
    }
  numberOfLinesInPaper = lineNumberInPaper;
}
```

Note that every paper/section iterative occurrence must be checked to verify that it is not Paper 139, Section 10, which is missing in *The Urantia Book* because in that paper, logical, structure-based Sections 10 and 11 are combined into one physical section; therefore, the convention in Urantia Book labeling is to proceed directly from Section 9 to Section 11, creating no section number 10 at all.

4

Programs

Overview

Programmers

The major constraint in Urantia Book programming—that is, in applying data processing techniques to Urantia Book text—is that, to my knowledge, no professional programmers and systems analysts have publicly identified themselves among the Urantia Book readership and no groups involved with Urantia Book dissemination have come forward to employ and support professional programmers and systems analysts; i.e., application designers, database designers, data engineers, data managers, data programmers, data technicians.

Consequently, no professional IT component exists to apply itself to studying, researching, analyzing, pamphletizing, and printing the Urantia Book.

Until a professional IT component arrives on the scene and is publicly brought into the staff of Urantia Foundation or another Urantia Book group of means, no significant Urantia Book-related programming or processing can be done.

Toolkit

The current Urantia Book Programming practice of coding all programs in script and employing the services of

Microsoft Internet Explorer or Google Chrome and the mechanism of hypertext applications (*.hta) was adopted to allow for programming with minimum programming skills and minimum budget. Also, when the first Urantia Book Programming application was developed, unicode capabilities were just barely coming to a few compilers and some interpreters.

Flat file data storage structure was chosen in order to allow more intuitive awareness of the data and less abstraction through mappings and tables.

ASCII character encoding was selected before non-english text was specified for Urantia Book Programming, to provide maximum awareness of the encoded content; that is, human readability. This character encoding was replaced by unicode—specifically, UTF-16LE—to facilitate multilingual capabilities.

Per-file header records were proscribed to avoid any possible source of confusion and, soon after multilingual capabilities were specified, even the descriptive prefixes designed for each record in the text files of the papers were eliminated.

Until such time as the current UBP practices have been implemented and running smoothly for a given Urantia Book data processing activity, as operated and maintained by IT professionals, they should be continued, and more sophisticated practices should be delayed.

Gradually the files at a given facility—exemplar files and metrics files—will be replaced by a single relational database that is designed, developed, and operated by experienced database engineers. Scripts and interpreted languages will be replaced by compiled languages and RDB stored procecures for writing utilities and for writing applications to transform, on a language-independent basis, data from the relational database into a large range of media in a variety of formats and languages. But the root design of these sophisticated techniques, I believe, must be based on, and remain patterned after, exemplar metrics techniques in some form or another.

These Urantia Book Programming operations can be carried out independently, in any country where there is a group willing and able to fund and manage the implementation of Urantia Book Programming techniques by IT professionals to translate the Urantia Book into their own and perhaps other languages and disseminate the translation or translations.

5

Paradigm

Protocol

The UBP Primary Protocol

The **UBP Primary Protocol** is the guiding decision-making factor behind the entire Urantia Book Programming Paradigm (the UBP Protocol and the Urantia Book Programming Language) and, further, of the designs, strategies, and coding of the UBP programs and systems.

The UBP Primary Protocol was adopted to compensate for the scarcity of resources and skillsets outside of myself. Should this situation improve, the UBP Primry Protocol should continue to be followed, but perhaps with decreased priority.

The UBP Primary Protocol is as follows:

1. Provide for maximum inherent human cognition.

2. Expect minimum resources and skillsets.

System Folders

There are 4 levels of system folders, as follows:

Level 1 Folder

The Urantia Book Data System has one Level 1 Folder. This folder, named *ubds,* contains the entire

Urantia Book Data System.

Level 2 Folders

There are two Level 2 Folders, and they are contained within the Level 1 Folder, *ubds*. They are named *data* and *processing*. The data they contain is as follows:

1. The Level 2 *data* folder.

   The top level folder for all of the *static* data of the ubds; that is, data files whose records are not in a state of incomplete editing and correction by Urantia Book Translator.

2. The Level 2 *processing* folder

   The folder containing the program folders; that is, the *urantiabooktranslator* folder and the *urantiabookcodifier* folder.

Level 3 Folders

The Level 3 Folders consist of six data folders, named for the six types of UBDS data files, in the Level 2 data folder, and two programming folders, urantiabookcodifier and urantiabooktranslator, in the Level 2 processing folder.

These eight Level 3 folders are as follows:

1. In the Level 2 *data* folder:

   1. arcexemplar

   2. exemplar

   3. import

   4. preimport

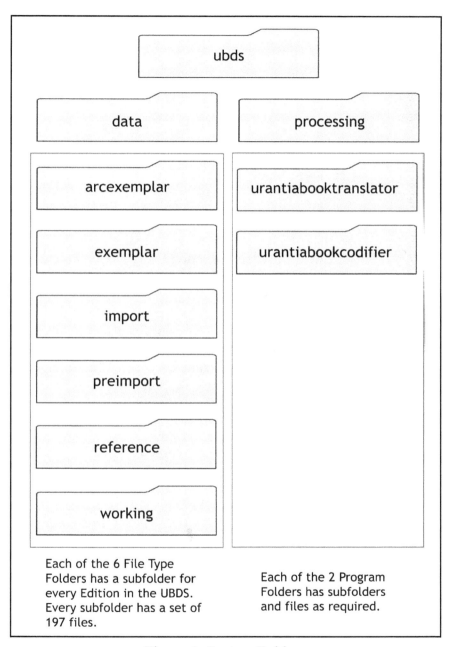

Figure 1. System Folders

> 5. reference
>
> 6. working

2. In the level 2 *processing* folder:

> 1. Urantia Book Translator
>
> 2. Urantia Book Codifier

Level 4 Folders

Each of the six Level 3 data folders contains an identical set of Level 4 Folders, one for each Edition of The Urantia Book stored in the UBDS. The Level 4 Folders are individually named for the Edition with which they are concerned, their names each consisting of the first of the three segments of the individual file names of the files they will hold, without the extension; for example, the Level 4 Folder containing the Russian edition of The Urantia Book translated by the Urantia Society of Greater New York in 2006 will be named *rusnys2006*, which is the first segment of the file name of every one of the files that it will contain.

The Level 3 *data* folder named *exemplar*, for example, might contain the Level 4 data folder named *rusnys2006*. If the corresponding reference files have been created, then the *reference* folder in the *data* folder will also have a *rusnys2006* subfolder.

The name of the exemplar file for Paper 15 of the rusnys2006 edition is would be:

rusnys2006_exemplar_p015.u16

and the name of the reference file for the same paper of the same edition would be:

File Formats

All files are flat files, accessed by Sequential Access Method. Records are character-encoded in plain text unicode, in the UTF-16LE unicode transformation.

Records represent numeric values as numeric characters.

Each record is terminated by CRLF.

Exemplar Files

Each exemplar file contains the text of one paper of The Urantia Book, one record per book line of the paper, in ascending order of line sequence in the first printing of The Urantia Book. A *book line*, as the term is used here, refers to any of the following:

1. A Paper title.

2. A section title.

3. A paragraph (a block of text having an indented first line),

In instances of lines that are *multiline* section titles, spanning two or more *physical* lines, each such multiline section title is counted as a *single line*. In the exemplarizing procedure, the physical line breaks of the first printing are represented, in the exemplar files, with manual line breaks as defined in the Urantia Book Programming Language.

Exemplar Records

Each sequential record in an exemplar file for a particular Urantia Book paper represents one book line of text from that paper, ending with a CRLF line delimiter, the records and their respective printed lines being in ascending sequential order.

Multiline section titles are counted as single lines, the physical line breaks of their book lines of the first printing of The Urantia Book being represented by UBPL line breaks.

Each exemplar record is constructed, character by character from left to right, of the following:

1. Open bracket.

2. One-based sequence number of the record in the file.

3. Close bracket.

4. One space.

5. The UBPL-distilled text of the original Urantia Book line.

6. Carriage return.

7. Line feed.

Metrics Records

Metrics tables, and resultant metrics records, are designed to facilitate optimum inputting, processing, and outputting.

Metrics design includes the use of coded metrics, where such coding will increase optimization.

Program Coding Language

JavaScript is the program coding language.

File Types

The UBDS has six types of files. Each of these file types has a file-type-specific folder in the data folder of the ubds folder. Within each file type folder is a folder for every edition of The Urantia Book, each edition folder containing 197 files, one for every paper in the edition.

Arcexemplar Files

Exemplar files that have been renamed and the *record-type* portion of their file names changed from *exemplar* to *arcexemplar*. Arcexemplar files are archival files and are kept in edition-specific subfolders inside the *arcexemplar* Level 3 Folder.

Exemplar Files

Completed working files that have been renamed and the *record-type* portion of their file names changed fom *working* to *exemplar*, Exemplar files are used, for example, to display in the *To Language*, or right, column of Urantia Book Translator. Exemplar files are the final language files, used as input. for example, to pre-print formatting programs or analysis programs. Exemplar files are kept in edition-specific subfolders inside the *exemplar* Level 3 Folder.

Import Files

Preimport files that have had their structure and text reshaped, approximately, into those of the anticipated exemplar files that they are ultimately to become, having the *record-type* portion of their file names changed from *preimport* to *import*. Import files are kept in edition-specific subfolders inside the *import* Level 3 Folder.

Preimport Files

Files for a given language, constructed by various means as a first approximation to exemplar files, one per paper in The Urantia Book. The records of preimport files are in the proper order, though some individual records may be split, or fused, and will have to be corrected later.

The records of preimport files have no prefixes or UPL distilling of their text, a condition that can be corrected by running the set of files for the edition through *Urantia Book Codifier* to produce *import files*.

Preimport files are kept in edition-specific subfolders inside the *preimport* Level 3 Folder.

Reference Files

Completed exemplar files that have been renamed and the *record-type* portion of their file names changed fom *exemplar* to *reference*. Reference files are used, for example, to display in the *From Language*, or left, column of Urantia Book Translator. Reference files are kept in edition-specific subfolders inside the *reference* Level 3 Folder.

Working Files

Translated Urantia Book text files that begin their existence as import files that have been renamed and the record-type portion of their file names changed from *import* to *working*. As working files, they are then shown, and edited, as necessary, in the *To Language*, or right, column of Urantia Book Translator. When all their errors have been corrected, all the files of their encompassing fileset are transformed into exemplar files by having the *record-type* portion of their file names changed from *working* to *exemplar*.

Working files are kept in edition-specific subfolders inside the *working* Level 3 Folder.

6

Libraries

Code Libraries

About the Code Libraries

In JavaScript programming, certain data might be used over and over again. In addition, certain logical operations might be performed repeatedly. These frequently used quantities and procedures can be arranged into what is termed *re-usable code*, which can be made accessible to various programs at any desired locations in their code, without the need to code them or repeat the code.

In the UBP, various JavaScript logical functions and also functions containing and accessing data, such as metrics, are written and gathered together in groups of shared commonality—for example, into a group that all have to do with creating a Urantia Book with *abs* paragraph reference numbers in web page format from exemplar files. This particular example group of functions would be stored in a separate file, called a *library file*, named for its contents; for example, *absHTML.js*.

Every UBP Program resides in a folder named for that program. Inside every UBP program folder is an include folder, named *inc*, in which the include files that will be used for that program are stored.

Urantia Book Translator resides in the *urantiabooktrans-*

lator folder. Inside this Urantia Book Translator program folder is an *inc* folder that contains the following files:

1. absmap.js

2. exemplarmap.js

3. languagemap.js

4. ubt_analyzer.js

The .js extension identifies the file as JavaScript code.

Inside the Urantia Book Translator program folder is a file named *UBTranslator.hta*. This *hypertext application file* contains the full JavaScript code for Urantia Book Translator, except the code that is in the include files in the *inc* folder. Launching this .hta file, for example by means of a double click on its icon in Windows Explorer, executes Urantia Book Translator.

The .hta file is really a file of HTML code whose

<head>

section contains an embedded

<hta>

tag followed by some embedded JavaScript code set off by a pair of

<script> </script>

tags.

The Urantia Book Translator .hta File

<!--

File Name: UBTranslator.hta

Urantia Book Translator

Copyright (C) 2007, 2009 Troy R. Bishop. All rights reserved.

Module UBTranslator.hta   last edit 2009-08-21 trb

LICENSE ------------------------

```
------------------------------------------------------------------------
-->
<HTML>
<head>
<meta http-equiv="Content-Type" content="text/
html;charset=UTF-8">
<style>
.reportitem {
    font-size:14px;
    text-align:center;
    border:solid 1px #000000;
    border-collapse:collapse;
    padding-left:15px;
    padding-right:15px;
}
.borderlessreportitem {
    font-size:14px;
    text-align:left;
    border-collapse:collapse;
}
.hangingIndent {
//    margin-left: 12px;
    text-indent: -12px;
}
</style>
```

<TITLE>Urantia Book Translator</TITLE>

[The <.hta tag>, as below, is necessary for any .hta file.]

```
<HTA:APPLICATION ID="oHTA"
    APPLICATIONNAME="Urantia Book Translator"
    BORDER="thick"
    BORDERSTYLE="raised"
    CAPTION="yes"
    ICON="./ico/ubtranslator.ico"
    MAXIMIZEBUTTON="yes"
    MINIMIZEBUTTON="yes"
    SHOWINTASKBAR="yes"
    SINGLEINSTANCE="yes"
    SYSMENU="yes"
    VERSION="1.0"
    WINDOWSTATE="maximize"/>
<style type="text/css">
body {
    background-color: threedface;
    font-family:Arial;
}
.enhancedemphasiscolor EM {color:red}
.enhancedemphasisreverse EM {color:white;back-
ground-color:black}
.nonenhancedemphasis EM {color:black}

.enhancedemphasiscolor U {color:red}
.enhancedemphasisreverse U {color:white;back-
ground-color:black}
```

```
.nonenhancedemphasis U {color:black}


.enhancedemphasiscolor B {color:red}

.enhancedemphasisreverse B {color:white;back-
ground-color:black}

.nonenhancedemphasis B {color:black}


.enhancedemphasiscolor STRONG {color:red}

.enhancedemphasisreverse STRONG {col-
or:white;background-color:black}

.nonenhancedemphasis STRONG {color:black}


/*this class is to be removed and hard-coded in the
html*/
.multilinetd {
    word-wrap:break-word;
    font-size:14px;
    font-weight:normal;
}
</style>
```

*[The four lines below load the include files and make them
part of the body of the JavaScript code.]*

```
<script src="./inc/languagemap.js"></script>
<script src="./inc/exemplarmap.js"></script>
<script src="./inc/absmap.js"></script>
<script src="./inc/ubt_analyzer.js"></script>
```

*[The lines following the <script> tag below, up until the
</script> tag, are the main JavaScript code.]*

```
<script>

function leaveError ()
  {
  return true;
  }

window.onError = leaveError();

//This is the Absolute Structure Map of The Urantia
Book
var absMapObj = new absMap();
var languageMapObj = new languageMap();

var currentReferenceTextDirection = "ltr";
var currentWorkingTextDirection = "ltr";

var currentReferenceLanguageCode = "";
var currentReferenceLanguageCode3 = "";
var currentWorkingLanguageCode = "";
var currentWorkingLanguageCode3 = "";


var script = new Array ();
var preservedImportTextSelection = false;
var setupItemNameArray =
  [
  "currentReferenceLanguageCode",
  "currentWorkingLanguageCode",
  "currentPaperNumber",
```

```
"currentReferenceFont",
"currentReferenceFontSize",
"currentWorkingFont",
"currentWorkingFontSize",
"currentTranslationDictionaryName"
];
```

[Skipping to the end of the more than 7,000 lines of the JavaScript code (the full code can be viewed by examining the freely available .hta file), here are the final lines of the .hta file:]

```
columnMode = "two column";
setButtonToInset(setTwoColumnObj);
setButtonToNormal(setReferenceFullScreenObj.
parentNode);
setButtonToNormal(setWorkingFullScreenObj.
parentNode);
initializeTranslationDictionaries();
preservedEditWindowSelection.preservedEdi-
tAreaObj = null;
preservedEditWindowSelection.preservedSelec-
tionStart = null;
preservedEditWindowSelection.preservedSelec-
tionEnd = null;
hideWaitBar();
}


//----------------------end functions------------------------


</script>
```

[This above completes the JavaScript code. Immediately following is more HTML code, starting with the below few lines:]

```
</HEAD>


<BODY id="bodytag"  STYLE="margin:0px-
;background-color:gray;overflow-Y:hidden;over-
flow-X:hidden" onResize="processOnResize()"
onLoad="initialize()" onBeforeUnload="proces-
sOnBeforeUnload()" oncontextmenu="return
false">


<!--Create the Dialog Helper Object-->
 <OBJECT ID=dlgHelper CLASSID="cl-
sid:3050f819-98b5-11cf-bb82-00aa00bdce0b"
WIDTH="0px" HEIGHT="0px"></OBJECT>


<!-- Create the licensing object for the common
dialog activex control -->
<OBJECT CLASSID="clsid:5220cb21-c88d-11cf-
b347-00aa00a28331">
   <PARAM NAME="LPKPath" VALUE="comdlg.
lpk">
</OBJECT>
```

[Skipping to the end of the HTML code, it ends with the following lines:]

```
<div id="yesnocancelbox" style="width:321px-
;height:115px;margin:0;position:abso-
lute;left:150px;top:200px;text-align:left;back-
ground-color:threedface;overflow:hidden;z-ind-
ex:2100;text-align:center;display:none;border:sol-
id activecaption 1px">
```

```
<div id="yesnocaptionbar" style="width:321px-
;height:29px;margin:0;text-align:left;back-
ground-color:activecaption;overflow:hidden">

<div id="yesnocancelclosebutton"
style="width:21px;height:100%;text-align:cen-
ter;vertical-align:center;display:inline;-
float:right;padding-right:2px"><img src="./gif/
system_close_button_21x21.gif" width="21"
height="21" border="0" onclick="processY-
esNoCancelBoxReturn('cancel')" style="mar-
gin-top:4px"></div>

<div id="yesnocancelcaption" style="width:290px-
;height:100%;text-align:left;display:inline;col-
or:white;font-size:12px;padding-top:6px;pad-
ding-left:4px">Urantia Book Translator</div>

</div>

<div id="yesnocanceltophalf"
style="width:100%;height:45px;text-align:center">

<div id="yesnocancelmessagediv"
style="width:250px;height:45px;text-align:cen-
ter;display:inline;float:right;font-size:12px;pad-
ding-top:14px">Do you want to save the changes
to the current Paper?</div>

<div id="yesnocanceltophalfleft"
style="width:65px;height:45px;display:inline;-
margin:0"><img src="./gif/exclamation_in_yel-
low_triangle_31x32.gif" width="31" height="32"
border="0" hspace="0" vspace="0" style="mar-
gin-top:9px"></div>

<div id="yesnocancelbottomhalf"
style="width:100%;height:100%;text-align:center">

<div style="width:58px;height:19px;back-
ground-color:threedface;border-left:groove;bor-
der-top:groove;border-right:ridge;bor-
der-bottom:ridge;font-size:12px;color:black;-
text-align:center;vertical-align:middle;dis-
play:inline;margin-top:4px;cursor:default"
onclick="processYesNoCancelBoxRe-
turn('yes')">Yes</div>
```

```
<div style="width:58px;height:19px;back-
ground-color:threedface;border-left:groove;bor-
der-top:groove;border-right:ridge;bor-
der-bottom:ridge;font-size:12px;col-
or:black;text-align:center;vertical-align:mid-
dle;display:inline;margin-left:16px;mar-
gin-right:16px;margin-top:4px;cursor:default"
onclick="processYesNoCancelBoxReturn('no')">-
No</div>

<div style="width:58px;height:19px;back-
ground-color:threedface;border-left:groove;bor-
der-top:groove;border-right:ridge;bor-
der-bottom:ridge;font-size:12px;color:black;-
text-align:center;vertical-align:middle;dis-
play:inline;margin-top:4px;cursor:default"
onclick="processYesNoCancelBoxReturn('can-
cel')">Cancel</div>

</div>

</div>

</div>

</BODY>

</HTML>
```

The absmap.js Code Library

```
/*
```

File Name: absmap.js

AbsoluteStructure Map of The Urantia Book
last edit 2010-02-04 trb

2009-12-02 - added 51:7 to list of multiline section titles

2010-01-02 - corrected absLineNumberInSectionIn-Paper(paperNumber, absSectionNumber, lineNumberInAbsSection)

2010-02-04 - added 148:42 to list of multiline section titles

----

This object contains the following public methods:

absLineNumberInExemplarSection (paperNum-ber, lineNumber)

absLineNumberInAbsSection (paperNumber, lineNumber)

absLineType (paperNumber, lineNumber)

absNumberOfLinesInAbsSection (paperNumber, absSectionNumber)

absNumberOfLinesInExemplarSection (paper-Number, exemplarSectionNumber)

absNumberOfSublinesInLine (paperNumber, lineNumber)

absNumberOfSublinesInLineBookwideArray ()

absSectionNumberOfLine (paperNumber, lineNumber)

absLineNumberInSectionInPaper(paperNumber, absSectionNumber, lineNumberInAbsSection)

exemplarSectionNumberToAbsSectionNumber

(paperNumber, exemplarSectionNumber)

absSectionNumberToExemplarSectionNumber = function (paperNumber, absSectionNumber)

expandAbsDataForPaperWhereNecessary (paperNumber)

lineIsAcknowledgmentHeading (paperNumber, lineNumberInPaper)

lineIsPaperTitle (lineNumberInPaper)

lineIsSectionTitle(paperNumber, lineNumberIn-Paper)

lineNumber, sectionNumber, and paperNumber are purely physical and are unmapped.

lineNumber is one-based and unmapped.

sectionNumber is zero-based and unmapped.

paperNumber is zero-based and unmapped.

----

*/

//this is the absMap constructor

function absMap ()

 {

// BEGIN (PRIVATE) PROPERTIES

 this.vcurrentAbsPaperNumber = null;

//Keyed on paperNumber:lineNumberInPaper, joined by a colon.

 this.vabsNumberOfSublinesInLineBookwideAr-ray =

  {

  "42:14" : 2,

  "42:118" : 2,

```
    "51:38" : 2,


    "57:67" : 2,
    "57:78" : 3,


    "59:11" : 2,
    "59:32" : 2,
    "59:46" : 2,
    "59:59" : 3,
    "59:78" : 3,
    "59:102" : 3,


    "60:35" : 3,


    "61:5" : 2,
    "61:20" : 2,
    "61:34" : 2,
    "61:50" : 2,


    "148:42" : 2
    };


    var absLineTypeNameArray =
      {
      "papertitle" : "papertitle",
      "sectiontitle" : "sectiontitle",
      "acknowledgmentheading" : "acknowledg-
    mentheading",
      "paragraph" : "paragraph"
      };
```

```
var absNumberOfSublinesInLinePaperwideArray
= [];
//-------------------------------------
//   END (PRIVATE) PROPERTIES
//   BEGIN METHODS
this.expandAbsDataForPaper = function (paper-
Number)
   {
   if (paperNumber == this.vcurrentAbsPaper-
Number)
      {
      return;
      }
   this.expandExemplarDataForPaperWhereNec-
essary(paperNumber);

   var sectionIndex = null;
   var lineIndex = null;
   var zeroIndex = null;
   var sublinesNumber = null;
   var sublinesQuantity = null;
   var splitKeyArray = null;
   var displayString = "";
   var sectionLineIndex = null;
   var lowSectionLineNumber = null;
   var highSectionLineNumber = null;
   var currentLineNumberInPaper = null;
   var lineNumberInSection = null;

   this.vcurrentAbsPaperNumber = paperNumber;
   sectionArray[0].absNumberOfSublinesInSec-
```

```
tionTitleLine = 0;
    sectionArray[0].absSectionNumber = 0;


    for (sectionIndex = 1; sectionIndex <= this.
vnumberOfSectionsInPaper; sectionIndex++)
        {
        //fill absSectionNumber property in section-
Array elements
        if (this.vcurrentAbsPaperNumber == 139 &&
sectionIndex > 9)
            {
            //adjustment because of original labeling
anomaly that skips labsSection 10 in Paper 139
            sectionArray[sectionIndex].absSection-
Number = sectionIndex + 1;
            }
        else
            {
            sectionArray[sectionIndex].absSection-
Number = sectionIndex;
            }
        //initialize absNumberOfSublinesInLine proper-
ty in sectionArray elements to 0
        sectionArray[sectionIndex].absNumberOf-
SublinesInSectionTitleLine = 0;
        }


    //set lineType for all lines to "paragraph" and
absNumberOfSublinesInLine to 0
    for (lineIndex = 1; lineIndex <= this.vnumberOf-
LinesInPaper; lineIndex++)
        {
        lineArray[lineIndex] = new Array();
```

```
        lineArray[lineIndex].absLineType = "para-
graph";
        lineArray[lineIndex].absNumberOfSublinesIn-
Line = 0;
        }


    //set line type for first line to "paperTitle"
    lineArray[1].AbslineType = "papertitle";


    //set line type for lines that contain section
titles to "sectionTitle"
    for (sectionIndex = 0; sectionIndex < this.
vnumberOfSectionsInPaper; sectionIndex++)

        {
        if (sectionIndex != 0)

            {
            lineArray[sectionArray[sectionIndex].
sectionTitleLineNumberInPaper].absLineType =
"sectiontitle";

                }


        lowSectionLineNumber = sectionArray[sec-
tionIndex].lowSectionLineNumberInPaper;

        highSectionLineNumber = sectionArray[sec-
tionIndex].highSectionLineNumberInPaper;


        lineNumberInSection = 0;
        //in lineArray, for each line set sectionNum-
berOfLine and labelSectionNumberOfLine

        for (sectionLineIndex = lowSectionLineNum-
ber; sectionLineIndex <= highSectionLineNumber;
sectionLineIndex++)

            {
            currentLineNumberInPaper = sectionArray[-
```

```
sectionIndex].sectionTitleLineNumberInPaper +
lineNumberInSection;


        //fill absSectionNumberOfLine property for
all lineArray elements in section
        if (paperNumber != 139 || currentLineNum-
berInPaper < 121)
            {
        lineArray[currentLineNumberInPaper].
absSectionNumberOfLine = sectionIndex;
            }
        else
            {
        //increase absSectionNumberOfLine by 1
because section 10 is skipped in abs structure
        lineArray[currentLineNumberInPaper].
absSectionNumberOfLine = sectionIndex + 1;
            }
        lineArray[currentLineNumberInPaper].sec-
tionNumberOfLine = sectionIndex;
        if (paperNumber == 0)
            {
        //fill in lineNumberInSection and
absLineNumberInSection for Paper 0
        if (currentLineNumberInPaper != 180)
            {
            lineNumberInSection++;
            }
        if (currentLineNumberInPaper == 181)
            {
        //line no. 181 in Paper 0 is not counted
in calculation of absLineNumberInSection
        lineArray[currentLineNumberInPaper].
```

```
            absLineNumberInSection = -1;
      }
   else
      {
      lineArray[currentLineNumberInPaper].
absLineNumberInSection = lineNumberInSection;
      }
   }
   else
      {
      lineArray[currentLineNumberInPaper].
absLineNumberInSection = lineNumberInSection;

      lineNumberInSection++;
      }
   }
}


if (this.vcurrentAbsPaperNumber == 0)
{
//set line type for the sole acknowledgment
heading to "acknowledgment heading"
   lineArray[181].absLineType = "acknowledg-
mentheading";
}


//fill number of sublines property in sectionAr-
ray elements and lineArray elements
for (sublinesNumber in this.vabsNumberOf-
SublinesInLineBookwideArray)
   {
   splitKeyArray = sublinesNumber.split(":");

   if (splitKeyArray[0] == this.vcurrentAbsPaper-
Number)
```

```
            {
            splitLineNumber = splitKeyArray[1];

            sublinesQuantity = this.vabsNumberOfSub-
linesInLineBookwideArray[sublinesNumber];

            lineArray[splitLineNumber].absNumberOf-
SublinesInLine = sublinesQuantity;

            sectionArray[lineArray[splitLineNumber].
sectionNumberOfLine].absNumberOfSublinesIn-
SectionTitleLine = sublinesQuantity;

            }
        }
    }


    this.absLineNumberInExemplarSection = func-
tion (paperNumber, lineNumber)
    {
    if (!this.paperNumberAndLineNumberAreValid(-
paperNumber, lineNumber))
        {
        return -1;
        }
    this.expandExemplarDataForPaperWhereNec-
essary(paperNumber);

    return lineArray[lineNumber].absLineNumber-
InSection;
    }


    this.absLineNumberInAbsSection = function
(paperNumber, lineNumber)
    {
    if (!this.paperNumberAndLineNumberAreValid(-
paperNumber, lineNumber))
        {
```

```
    return -1;
    }
this.expandExemplarDataForPaperWhereNec-
essary(paperNumber);
    return lineArray[lineNumber].absLineNumber-
InSection;
    }


this.absLineType = function (paperNumber,
lineNumber)
    {
    if (!this.paperNumberAndLineNumberAreValid(-
paperNumber, lineNumber))
    {
    return -1;
    }
this.expandExemplarDataForPaperWhereNec-
essary(paperNumber);
    if (paperNumber == 0 && lineNumber == 181)
    {
    return "acknowledgmentheading";
    }
    else
    {
    return this.lineType(paperNumber, lineNum-
ber);
    }
    }


this.absNumberOfLinesInAbsSection = function
(paperNumber, absSectionNumber)
    {
    if (paperNumber == 139 && absSectionNumber
```

```
> 9)
    {
    return this.absNumberOfLinesInExemplar-
Section(paperNumber, absSectionNumber - 1);
    }
    else
    {
    return this.absNumberOfLinesInExemplar-
Section(paperNumber, absSectionNumber);
    }
    }


  this.absNumberOfLinesInExemplarSection =
function (paperNumber, exemplarSectionNumber)
    {
    if (paperNumber < 0 || paperNumber > 196 ||
exemplarSectionNumber < 0 || exemplarSection-
Number > this.exemplarSectionSizeArray[paper-
Number].length - 1)
    {
    return -1;
    }
    var numberOfLines = this.numberOfLinesIn-
Section(paperNumber, exemplarSectionNumber);
    if (paperNumber == 0 && exemplarSectionNum-
ber == 12)
    {
    return numberOfLines - 1;
    }
    else
    {
    return numberOfLines;
    }
```

```
        }

    this.absNumberOfSublinesInLine = function
(paperNumber, lineNumber)
    {
    if (!this.paperNumberAndLineNumberAreValid(-
paperNumber, lineNumber))
        {
        return -1;
        }
    this.expandExemplarDataForPaperWhereNec-
essary(paperNumber);
    var sublinesCount = this.vabsNumberOfSub-
linesInLineBookwideArray[paperNumber + ":" +
lineNumber];
    return sublinesCount == null ? 0 : subline-
sCount;
        }


    this.absNumberOfSublinesInLineBookwideArray
= function ()
    {
    var arrayForReturn = new Array();
    for (var sublinesNumber in this.vabsNumberOf-
SublinesInLineBookwideArray)
        {
        arrayForReturn[sublinesNumber] = this.
vabsNumberOfSublinesInLineBookwideArray[sub-
linesNumber];
        }
    return arrayForReturn;
        }
```

```
this.absSectionNumberOfLine = function (paper-
Number, lineNumber)

{

if (!this.paperNumberAndLineNumberAreValid(-
paperNumber, lineNumber))

{

return -1;

}

this.expandExemplarDataForPaperWhereNec-
essary(paperNumber);

return this.sectionNumberOfLine(paperNum-
ber, lineNumber);

}


this.absLineNumberInSectionInPaper = function
(paperNumber, absSectionNumber, lineNumber-
InAbsSection)

{

this.expandExemplarDataForPaperWhereNec-
essary(paperNumber);

var exemplarSectionNumber =  this.absSec-
tionNumberToExemplarSectionNumber(paperNum-
ber, absSectionNumber, lineNumberInAbsSection);

var baseLineNumber = this.lineNumberInPap-
erOfSectionTitle(paperNumber, exemplarSection-
Number);

return parseInt(baseLineNumber) + par-
seInt(lineNumberInAbsSection);

}


this.exemplarSectionNumberToAbsSectionNum-
ber = function (paperNumber, exemplarSection-
Number)

{
```

```
        if (paperNumber < 0 || paperNumber > 196 ||
exemplarSectionNumber < 0 || exemplarSection-
Number > this.exemplarSectionSizeArray[paper-
Number].length - 1)
    {
    return -1;
    }
    return paperNumber == 139 && exemplarSec-
tionNumber > 9 ? exemplarSectionNumber + 1 :
exemplarSectionNumber;
    }


    this.absSectionNumberToExemplarSectionNum-
ber = function (paperNumber, absSectionNumber)
    {
    if (paperNumber < 0 || paperNumber > 196 )
    {
    return -1;
    }
    return paperNumber == 139 && absSection-
Number > 9 ? absSectionNumber - 1 : absSection-
Number;
    }


    this.expandAbsDataForPaperWhereNecessary =
function (paperNumber)
    {
    if (this.vcurrentAbsPaperNumber != paperNum-
ber)
    {
    this.expandAbsDataForPaper(paperNumber);
    }
    }
```

```
this.lineIsAcknowledgmentHeading = function
(paperNumber, lineNumberInPaper)
    {
    if (!this.paperNumberAndLineNumberAreValid(-
paperNumber, lineNumberInPaper))
        {
        return -1;
        }
    return paperNumber == 0 && lineNumberInPa-
per == 181;
    }


this.lineIsPaperTitle = function (lineNumberInPa-
per)
    {
    return lineNumberInPaper == 1;
    }


this.lineIsSectionTitle = function (paperNumber,
lineNumberInPaper)
    {
    if (!this.paperNumberAndLineNumberAreValid(-
paperNumber, lineNumberInPaper))
        {
        return -1;
        }
    this.expandExemplarDataForPaperWhereNec-
essary(paperNumber);
    return this.lineType(paperNumber, lineNumber-
InPaper) == "sectiontitle";
    }
```

```
    this.lineIsSectionTitle = function (paperNumber,
lineNumberInPaper)

    {

    if (!this.paperNumberAndLineNumberAreValid(-
paperNumber, lineNumberInPaper))

      {

      return -1;

      }

    this.expandExemplarDataForPaperWhereNec-
essary(paperNumber);

    return this.lineType(paperNumber, lineNumber-
InPaper) == "sectiontitle";

      }

  }


// inherit exemplarMap

    absMap.prototype = new exemplarMap();

//----------------------------------------------
```

The exemplarmap.js Code Library

```
/*

File Name: exemplarmap.js

-------------------------------------------------

Exemplar Structure Map of The Urantia Book
last edit 2010-01-02 trb

Copyright (C) 2007, 2009 Troy R. Bishop.  All rights
reserved.

LICENSE --------------------------

Permission is hereby granted, free of charge, to
any person obtaining a copy

of this software and associated documentation
files (the "Software"), to deal

in the Software without restriction, including with-
out limitation the rights

to use, copy, modify, merge, publish, distribute,
sublicense, and/or sell

copies of the Software, and to permit persons to
whom the Software is

furnished to do so, subject to the following condi-
tions:


The above copyright notice and this permission
notice shall be included in

all copies or substantial portions of the Software.


THE SOFTWARE IS PROVIDED "AS IS", WITHOUT
WARRANTY OF ANY KIND, EXPRESS OR

IMPLIED, INCLUDING BUT NOT LIMITED TO THE
WARRANTIES OF MERCHANTABILITY,

FITNESS FOR A PARTICULAR PURPOSE AND
NONINFRINGEMENT. IN NO EVENT SHALL THE

AUTHORS OR COPYRIGHT HOLDERS BE LIABLE
FOR ANY CLAIM, DAMAGES OR OTHER
```

LIABILITY, WHETHER IN AN ACTION OF CON-
TRACT, TORT OR OTHERWISE, ARISING FROM,

OUT OF OR IN CONNECTION WITH THE SOFT-
WARE OR THE USE OR OTHER DEALINGS IN
THE SOFTWARE.

This object contains the following public methods:

expandExemplarDataForPaperWhereNecessary
(paperNumber)

lineNumberInSection (paperNumber, lineNumber)

lineType (paperNumber, lineNumber)

numberOfLinesInPaper (paperNumber)

numberOfLinesInSection (paperNumber, section-
Number)

numberOfSectionsInPaper (paperNumber)

paperNumberAndLineNumberAreValid (paper-
Number, lineNumber)

sectionNumberOfLine (paperNumber, lineNumber)

lineNumberInPaperOfSectionTitle (paperNumber,
sectionNumber);

lineNumber, sectionNumber, and paperNumber
are purely physical and are unmapped.

lineNumber is one-based and unmapped.

sectionNumber is zero-based and unmapped.

paperNumber is zero-based and unmapped.

----

*/

//this is the exemplarMap constructor
function exemplarMap ()

```
{

//  BEGIN PROPERTIES
   this.vcurrentPaperNumber = null;
   this.vnumberOfSectionsInPaper = null;
   this.vnumberOfLinesInPaper = null;
   this.lineArray = new Array();
   this.sectionArray = new Array();
   this.exemplarSectionSizeArray =
[
/* Paper0 */  [6, 26, 18, 25, 13, 12, 13, 10, 12, 5, 2,
16, 14],
/* Paper1 */  [6, 6, 10, 8, 7, 16, 8, 9],
/* Paper2 */  [3, 11, 7, 6, 5, 12, 9, 13],
/* Paper3 */  [3, 12, 15, 5, 7, 17, 9],
/* Paper4 */  [3, 12, 8, 7, 9, 8],
/* Paper5 */  [2, 12, 6, 8, 15, 14, 14],
/* Paper6 */  [4, 6, 8, 5, 10, 7, 4, 3, 9],
/* Paper7 */  [5, 11, 4, 7, 7, 11, 8, 7],
/* Paper8 */  [4, 11, 8, 9, 8, 6, 8],
/* Paper9 */  [5, 8, 5, 8, 6, 7, 9, 5, 26],
/* Paper10 */  [3, 6, 8, 19, 7, 8, 18, 6, 10],
/* Paper11 */  [2, 4, 11, 4, 5, 9, 5, 9, 9, 9],
/* Paper12 */  [3, 16, 6, 12, 16, 11, 13, 14, 16, 7],
/* Paper13 */  [7, 23, 10, 3, 8],
/* Paper14 */  [2, 18, 9, 8, 22, 11, 42],
/* Paper15 */  [3, 6, 25, 16, 9, 14, 16, 12, 10, 18, 23,
3, 4, 6, 10],
/* Paper16 */  [12, 4, 5, 20, 16, 5, 11, 10, 19, 16],
/* Paper17 */  [12, 10, 6, 11, 3, 5, 10, 1, 10],
/* Paper18 */  [11, 6, 4, 9, 9, 5, 7, 6],
```

```
/* Paper19 */   [9, 12, 6, 7, 9, 12, 8, 6],
/* Paper20 */   [5, 15, 9, 4, 5, 7, 9, 5, 4, 5, 5],
/* Paper21 */   [5, 4, 12, 24, 6, 10, 5],
/* Paper22 */   [5, 15, 9, 4, 7, 6, 3, 14, 6, 8, 10],
/* Paper23 */   [2, 10, 24, 9, 7],
/* Paper24 */   [11, 16, 9, 4, 3, 5, 9, 10],
/* Paper25 */   [9, 7, 12, 17, 20, 4, 6, 4, 12],
/* Paper26 */   [1, 17, 7, 10, 15, 6, 4, 6, 5, 4, 7, 9],
/* Paper27 */   [11, 5, 3, 4, 4, 5, 6, 11],
/* Paper28 */   [6, 3, 2, 2, 14, 22, 22, 5],
/* Paper29 */   [11, 4, 19, 12, 38, 8],
/* Paper30 */   [2, 114, 157, 13, 35],
/* Paper31 */   [13, 5, 4, 8, 1, 3, 2, 5, 4, 14, 22],
/* Paper32 */   [4, 5, 13, 15, 12, 9],
/* Paper33 */   [1, 5, 5, 8, 8, 4, 9, 8, 7],
/* Paper34 */   [3, 4, 6, 8, 13, 7, 13, 9],
/* Paper35 */   [7, 4, 9, 22, 5, 7, 5, 3, 15, 10, 6],
/* Paper36 */   [1, 4, 20, 9, 8, 17, 8],
/* Paper37 */   [2, 10, 11, 8, 5, 11, 7, 2, 10, 12, 7],
/* Paper38 */   [3, 3, 6, 1, 4, 4, 3, 7, 6, 14],
/* Paper39 */   [11, 18, 18, 11, 18, 17, 9, 2, 10, 4],
/* Paper40 */   [11, 2, 2, 1, 2, 19, 8, 5, 5, 9, 15],
/* Paper41 */   [4, 5, 8, 10, 7, 8, 7, 15, 4, 5, 6],
/* Paper42 */   [2, 9, 23, 13, 14, 16, 8, 10, 7, 5, 7, 8,
16],
/* Paper43 */   [4, 11, 8, 8, 10, 17, 8, 5, 13, 6],
/* Paper44 */   [21, 15, 11, 9, 12, 10, 9, 4, 7],
/* Paper45 */   [3, 11, 6, 22, 21, 7, 9, 9],
/* Paper46 */   [1, 9, 9, 4, 9, 33, 12, 8, 5],
/* Paper47 */   [4, 6, 8, 12, 8, 3, 4, 5, 7, 5, 8],
/* Paper48 */   [3, 7, 26, 18, 20, 10, 37, 31, 5],
```

/* Paper49 */ [5, 7, 26, 6, 9, 32, 22],

/* Paper50 */ [2, 4, 7, 6, 13, 11, 5, 4],

/* Paper51 */ [3, 8, 4, 9, 8, 7, 13, 6],

/* Paper52 */ [9, 8, 12, 12, 10, 10, 8, 17],

/* Paper53 */ [2, 6, 5, 7, 7, 7, 6, 15, 9, 9],

/* Paper54 */ [2, 10, 5, 3, 8, 14, 11],

/* Paper55 */ [12, 6, 12, 22, 31, 6, 10, 4, 7, 3, 11, 8, 6],

/* Paper56 */ [2, 6, 3, 6, 5, 4, 5, 9, 4, 14, 23],

/* Paper57 */ [2, 7, 4, 12, 9, 14, 11, 10, 27],

/* Paper58 */ [1, 8, 10, 5, 4, 8, 8, 13],

/* Paper59 */ [9, 20, 13, 12, 18, 23, 13],

/* Paper60 */ [2, 14, 15, 22, 7],

/* Paper61 */ [3, 14, 13, 15, 7, 8, 4, 20],

/* Paper62 */ [1, 3, 6, 13, 7, 11, 6, 8],

/* Paper63 */ [3, 4, 7, 6, 9, 7, 9, 5],

/* Paper64 */ [2, 8, 7, 5, 13, 4, 35, 21],

/* Paper65 */ [7, 9, 16, 7, 12, 4, 10, 8, 7],

/* Paper66 */ [2, 5, 9, 8, 16, 31, 7, 20, 8],

/* Paper67 */ [1, 6, 6, 10, 7, 5, 10, 8, 6],

/* Paper68 */ [3, 7, 11, 5, 7, 13, 12],

/* Paper69 */ [3, 6, 7, 11, 8, 15, 8, 5, 12, 19],

/* Paper70 */ [3, 22, 21, 11, 10, 9, 6, 19, 18, 17, 16, 14, 21],

/* Paper71 */ [2, 24, 19, 12, 17, 4, 3, 13, 16],

/* Paper72 */ [3, 5, 17, 9, 6, 12, 9, 14, 7, 8, 3, 5, 6],

/* Paper73 */ [3, 7, 5, 6, 5, 8, 8, 5],

/* Paper74 */ [1, 6, 8, 10, 6, 8, 9, 24, 15],

/* Paper75 */ [1, 6, 5, 9, 8, 9, 4, 7, 8],

/* Paper76 */ [2, 4, 9, 10, 8, 7, 5],

/* Paper77 */ [2, 7, 12, 9, 13, 10, 6, 8, 13, 13],

/* Paper78 */ [2, 13, 5, 10, 6, 8, 8, 7, 13],
/* Paper79 */ [1, 9, 8, 8, 9, 9, 13, 6, 18],
/* Paper80 */ [2, 8, 5, 9, 6, 8, 5, 13, 5, 17],
/* Paper81 */ [2, 8, 20, 8, 14, 7, 45],
/* Paper82 */ [3, 10, 5, 15, 5, 10, 12],
/* Paper83 */ [3, 5, 6, 4, 9, 15, 8, 9, 10],
/* Paper84 */ [3, 9, 7, 10, 11, 14, 8, 30, 7],
/* Paper85 */ [4, 5, 6, 5, 4, 3, 5, 4],
/* Paper86 */ [2, 6, 7, 4, 8, 17, 7, 7],
/* Paper87 */ [2, 5, 10, 5, 7, 14, 17, 11],
/* Paper88 */ [2, 10, 10, 4, 8, 5, 9],
/* Paper89 */ [2, 7, 5, 7, 10, 16, 8, 5, 8, 4, 7],
/* Paper90 */ [3, 6, 13, 10, 9, 9],
/* Paper91 */ [5, 6, 8, 7, 5, 7, 7, 13, 13, 9],
/* Paper92 */ [5, 5, 6, 10, 9, 16, 20, 16],
/* Paper93 */ [2, 3, 8, 8, 16, 14, 8, 4, 1, 11, 12],
/* Paper94 */ [1, 7, 8, 8, 10, 8, 12, 8, 19, 6, 3, 13, 8],
/* Paper95 */ [1, 11, 10, 5, 5, 15, 9, 7],
/* Paper96 */ [3, 15, 5, 5, 9, 9, 4, 9],
/* Paper97 */ [2, 10, 3, 6, 7, 6, 4, 14, 7, 29, 9],
/* Paper98 */ [4, 6, 12, 9, 8, 5, 5, 13],
/* Paper99 */ [3, 6, 6, 16, 13, 11, 4, 6],
/* Paper100 */ [2, 9, 8, 7, 6, 11, 9, 19],
/* Paper101 */ [3, 7, 17, 18, 10, 14, 17, 6, 4, 9, 10],
/* Paper102 */ [3, 6, 9, 15, 6, 3, 10, 10, 8],
/* Paper103 */ [7, 6, 10, 5, 5, 12, 15, 15, 6, 13],
/* Paper104 */ [3, 13, 6, 18, 47, 13],
/* Paper105 */ [3, 8, 11, 10, 9, 10, 5, 19],
/* Paper106 */ [19, 4, 8, 5, 4, 4, 6, 10, 23, 13],
/* Paper107 */ [7, 7, 9, 10, 7, 6, 7, 8],
/* Paper108 */ [2, 9, 11, 10, 5, 10, 9],

/* Paper109 */ [1, 5, 11, 8, 6, 5, 7, 9],
/* Paper110 */ [2, 6, 6, 10, 6, 7, 22, 11],
/* Paper111 */ [7, 9, 10, 7, 12, 6, 10, 6],
/* Paper112 */ [16, 19, 20, 7, 13, 22, 10, 20],
/* Paper113 */ [2, 8, 10, 6, 6, 5, 10, 9],
/* Paper114 */ [11, 4, 6, 5, 5, 6, 20, 18],
/* Paper115 */ [1, 4, 4, 19, 7, 2, 8, 9],
/* Paper116 */ [5, 5, 14, 6, 12, 17, 8, 7],
/* Paper117 */ [4, 9, 9, 13, 14, 14, 27, 18],
/* Paper118 */ [13, 10, 5, 7, 7, 3, 8, 8, 11, 9, 24],
/* Paper119 */ [7, 6, 7, 8, 6, 5, 6, 8, 9],
/* Paper120 */ [9, 7, 9, 12, 6],
/* Paper121 */ [1, 9, 12, 10, 6, 18, 9, 12, 14],
/* Paper122 */ [3, 3, 8, 4, 4, 11, 3, 8, 7, 28, 4],
/* Paper123 */ [6, 7, 16, 10, 9, 15, 9],
/* Paper124 */ [1, 13, 10, 10, 9, 6, 18],
/* Paper125 */ [7, 5, 12, 2, 4, 10, 13],
/* Paper126 */ [4, 7, 8, 14, 9, 12],
/* Paper127 */ [4, 8, 12, 15, 10, 6, 16],
/* Paper128 */ [5, 15, 7, 9, 9, 9, 12, 14],
/* Paper129 */ [3, 15, 11, 9, 8],
/* Paper130 */ [7, 6, 10, 10, 15, 4, 6, 8, 6],
/* Paper131 */ [2, 9, 13, 7, 8, 5, 2, 3, 6, 4, 8],
/* Paper132 */ [10, 4, 10, 11, 8, 25, 3, 9],
/* Paper133 */ [3, 5, 5, 12, 14, 12, 7, 13, 4, 6],
/* Paper134 */ [2, 7, 5, 8, 10, 17, 16, 7, 10, 9],
/* Paper135 */ [5, 4, 4, 4, 6, 8, 8, 3, 7, 9, 3, 4, 7],
/* Paper136 */ [2, 6, 8, 7, 14, 6, 11, 4, 8, 13, 1],
/* Paper137 */ [1, 8, 9, 7, 17, 4, 6, 14, 18],
/* Paper138 */ [2, 5, 10, 8, 4, 4, 5, 7, 11, 3, 11],
/* Paper139 */ [4, 12, 15, 9, 15, 12, 9, 10, 13, 11, 11,

14],
/* Paper140 */ [3, 7, 3, 21, 11, 24, 14, 8, 32, 4, 10],
/* Paper141 */ [2, 5, 3, 8, 9, 4, 5, 15, 3, 3],
/* Paper142 */ [2, 7, 5, 23, 4, 5, 9, 17, 5],
/* Paper143 */ [2, 9, 8, 8, 3, 13, 6, 9],
/* Paper144 */ [3, 10, 6, 23, 11, 102, 13, 4, 8, 2],
/* Paper145 */ [3, 3, 17, 15, 3, 10],
/* Paper146 */ [2, 4, 18, 11, 6, 3, 4, 3],
/* Paper147 */ [2, 4, 4, 6, 10, 10, 6, 3, 6],
/* Paper148 */ [5, 4, 5, 5, 11, 5, 12, 4, 5, 4],
/* Paper149 */ [4, 9, 14, 3, 6, 5, 12, 3],
/* Paper150 */ [4, 3, 3, 12, 4, 5, 3, 4, 11, 5],
/* Paper151 */ [2, 5, 8, 16, 7, 7, 8],
/* Paper152 */ [3, 5, 10, 3, 4, 6, 6, 3],
/* Paper153 */ [3, 7, 13, 7, 6, 5],
/* Paper154 */ [3, 3, 5, 2, 6, 4, 12, 5],
/* Paper155 */ [1, 6, 3, 8, 2, 16, 19],
/* Paper156 */ [2, 8, 8, 2, 3, 23, 10],
/* Paper157 */ [2, 5, 2, 7, 8, 3, 15, 5],
/* Paper158 */ [2, 10, 5, 6, 8, 5, 6, 9, 2],
/* Paper159 */ [2, 7, 4, 14, 11, 17, 5],
/* Paper160 */ [1, 15, 10, 5, 16, 14],
/* Paper161 */ [2, 11, 12, 3],
/* Paper162 */ [4, 11, 10, 5, 4, 5, 4, 6, 3, 7],
/* Paper163 */ [2, 6, 11, 7, 17, 3, 8, 4],
/* Paper164 */ [2, 4, 4, 16, 12, 6],
/* Paper165 */ [4, 3, 12, 9, 14, 7, 4],
/* Paper166 */ [2, 11, 8, 8, 12, 7],
/* Paper167 */ [3, 5, 4, 6, 7, 8, 6, 7],
/* Paper168 */ [12, 15, 10, 7, 13, 3],
/* Paper169 */ [7, 16, 8, 3, 13],

/* Paper170 */ [2, 17, 25, 11, 16, 21],
/* Paper171 */ [7, 6, 6, 5, 9, 3, 4, 10, 15],
/* Paper172 */ [3, 9, 5, 16, 3, 13],
/* Paper173 */ [3, 11, 8, 4, 5, 6],
/* Paper174 */ [3, 5, 5, 5, 7, 14],
/* Paper175 */ [2, 25, 3, 3, 15],
/* Paper176 */ [2, 7, 9, 10, 7],
/* Paper177 */ [4, 6, 7, 8, 12, 6],
/* Paper178 */ [1, 18, 12, 6],
/* Paper179 */ [5, 8, 3, 10, 8, 10],
/* Paper180 */ [3, 6, 7, 10, 6, 12, 9],
/* Paper181 */ [2, 10, 31],
/* Paper182 */ [2, 26, 13, 11],
/* Paper183 */ [5, 2, 4, 10, 8, 5],
/* Paper184 */ [3, 9, 13, 19, 6, 11],
/* Paper185 */ [4, 9, 16, 9, 3, 13, 7, 5, 2],
/* Paper186 */ [3, 7, 11, 5, 5, 9],
/* Paper187 */ [4, 11, 9, 6, 8, 8, 3],
/* Paper188 */ [3, 8, 3, 16, 13, 13],
/* Paper189 */ [3, 13, 9, 5, 14, 5],
/* Paper190 */ [5, 10, 7, 3, 2, 8],
/* Paper191 */ [13, 5, 2, 4, 7, 7, 4],
/* Paper192 */ [5, 11, 14, 3, 8],
/* Paper193 */ [6, 3, 3, 3, 14, 5, 6],
/* Paper194 */ [7, 5, 20, 20, 13],
/* Paper195 */ [18, 11, 9, 11, 5, 14, 17, 23, 13, 11, 21],
/* Paper196 */ [14, 13, 11, 35]
];

this.lineTypeNameArray =

```
        {
        "papertitle" : "papertitle",
        "sectiontitle" : "sectiontitle",
        "paragraph" : "paragraph"
        };
//-----------------------------------------------
//    END PROPERTIES

//    BEGIN METHODS
   this.expandExemplarDataForPaper = function
(paperNumber)
        {
        if (paperNumber == this.vcurrentPaperNumber)
          {
          return;
          }
        var sectionIndex = null;
        var lineIndex = null;
        var zeroIndex = null;
        var sectionLineIndex = null;
        var lowSectionLineNumber = null;
        var highSectionLineNumber = null;
        var lineArrayNumber = null;
//      var currentLineNumberInPaper = null;
        var lineNumberInSection = null;
        this.vcurrentPaperNumber = paperNumber;
        this.lineArray = [];
        this.sectionArray = [];
        this.vnumberOfLinesInPaper = this.numberOf-
LinesInPaper(this.vcurrentPaperNumber);
        this.vnumberOfSectionsInPaper = this.exem-
```

```
plarSectionSizeArray[this.vcurrentPaperNumber].
length;
    this.sectionArray[0] = new Array();
    this.sectionArray[0].sectionTitleLineNumberIn-
Paper = 1;
    this.sectionArray[0].sectionNumber = 0;
    this.sectionArray[0].lowSectionLineNumberIn-
Paper = 1;


    for (sectionIndex = 1; sectionIndex <= this.
vnumberOfSectionsInPaper; sectionIndex++)
    {
    //fill lineNumber property in sectionArray
elements
    this.sectionArray[sectionIndex] = new
Array();
    this.sectionArray[sectionIndex].sectionTitle-
LineNumberInPaper = this.sectionArray[sectionIn-
dex - 1].sectionTitleLineNumberInPaper + this.
exemplarSectionSizeArray[this.vcurrentPaper-
Number][sectionIndex - 1] + 1;
    this.sectionArray[sectionIndex].sectionNum-
ber = sectionIndex;
    this.sectionArray[sectionIndex].lowSection-
LineNumberInPaper = this.sectionArray[sectionIn-
dex].sectionTitleLineNumberInPaper;
    this.sectionArray[sectionIndex - 1].highSec-
tionLineNumberInPaper = this.sectionArray[sec-
tionIndex].sectionTitleLineNumberInPaper- 1;
    //initialize numberOfSublinesInLine property in
sectionArray elements to 0
    this.sectionArray[sectionIndex].numberOf-
SublinesInLine = 0;
    }
    this.sectionArray[this.vnumberOfSectionsIn-
Paper - 1].highSectionLineNumberInPaper = this.
```

```
    vnumberOfLinesInPaper;


    //set lineType for all lines to "paragraph" and
numberOfSublinesInLine to 0
    for (lineIndex = 1; lineIndex <= this.vnumberOf-
LinesInPaper; lineIndex++)
        {
        this.lineArray[lineIndex] = new Array();
        this.lineArray[lineIndex].lineType = "para-
graph";
        }


    //set line type for first line to "paperTitle"
    this.lineArray[1].lineType = "papertitle";


    //set line type for lines that contain section
titles to "sectionTitle"
    for (sectionIndex = 0; sectionIndex < this.
vnumberOfSectionsInPaper; sectionIndex++)
        {
        if (sectionIndex != 0)
            {
            lineArrayNumber = this.sectionArray[sec-
tionIndex].sectionTitleLineNumberInPaper;
                this.lineArray[lineArrayNumber].lineType =
"sectiontitle";
            }


        lowSectionLineNumber = this.sectionArray[-
sectionIndex].lowSectionLineNumberInPaper;
        highSectionLineNumber = this.sectionArray[-
sectionIndex].highSectionLineNumberInPaper;
```

```
        lineNumberInSection = 0;

    //in lineArray, for each line set sectionNum-
berOfLine and labelSectionNumberOfLine

        for (sectionLineIndex = lowSectionLineNum-
ber; sectionLineIndex <= highSectionLineNumber;
sectionLineIndex++)

            {

        currentLineNumberInPaper = this.section-
Array[sectionIndex].sectionTitleLineNumberInPa-
per + lineNumberInSection;

            this.lineArray[currentLineNumberInPaper].
sectionNumberOfLine = sectionIndex;

            this. lineArray[currentLineNumberInPaper].
lineNumberInSection = lineNumberInSection;

        lineNumberInSection++;

            }

        }

    }


    this.expandExemplarDataForPaperWhereNeces-
sary = function (paperNumber)

    {

    if (paperNumber != this.vcurrentPaperNumber)

        {

        this.expandExemplarDataForPaper(paper-
Number);

        }

    }


    this.lineNumberInSection = function (paperNum-
ber, lineNumber)

    {

    if (!this.paperNumberAndLineNumberAreValid(-
paperNumber, lineNumber))
```

```
        {
        return -1;
        }
    if (this.vcurrentPaperNumber != paperNumber)
        {
        this.expandExemplarDataForPaper(paper-
Number)
        }
    return this.lineArray[lineNumber].lineNumber-
InSection;
        }


  this.lineType = function (paperNumber, lineNum-
ber)
    {
    if (!this.paperNumberAndLineNumberAreValid(-
paperNumber, lineNumber))
        {
        return -1;
        }
    if (this.vcurrentPaperNumber != paperNumber)
        {
        this.expandExemplarDataForPaper(paper-
Number);
        }
    return this.lineArray[lineNumber].lineType;
        }


  this.numberOfLinesInPaper = function (paper-
Number)
    {
    if (paperNumber < 0 || paperNumber > 196)
```

```
    {
    return -1;
    }
//paper title is first line
var linesInPaper = 1;
//add number of paragraphs in each section
for (var sectionIndex = 0; sectionIndex < this.
exemplarSectionSizeArray[paperNumber].length;
sectionIndex++)
    {
    linesInPaper += this.exemplarSectionSizeAr-
ray[paperNumber][sectionIndex];
    }
//add 1 for each section title line except for
Sectin 0, which has no title line
    linesInPaper += this.exemplarSectionSizeAr-
ray[paperNumber].length - 1;
    return linesInPaper;
    }


  this.numberOfLinesInSection = function (paper-
Number, sectionNumber)
    {
    if (paperNumber < 0 || paperNumber > 196 ||
sectionNumber < 0 || sectionNumber > this.exem-
plarSectionSizeArray[paperNumber].length - 1)
    {
    return -1;
    }
    return this.exemplarSectionSizeArray[paper-
Number][sectionNumber];
    }
```

```
this.numberOfSectionsInPaper = function (paper-
Number)
  {
  if (paperNumber < 0 || paperNumber > 196)
    {
    return -1;
    }
  return this.exemplarSectionSizeArray[paper-
Number].length;
  }


this.paperNumberAndLineNumberAreValid =
function (paperNumber, lineNumber)
  {
  if (paperNumber < 0 || paperNumber > 196 ||
lineNumber < 1)
    {
    return 0;
    }
  return 1;
  }


this.sectionNumberOfLine = function (paperNum-
ber, lineNumber)
  {
  if (!this.paperNumberAndLineNumberAreValid(-
paperNumber, lineNumber))
    {
    return -1;
    }
  if (this.currentPaperNumber != paperNumber)
    {
```

```
        this.expandExemplarDataForPaper(paper-
Number)
    }
    return this.lineArray[lineNumber].sectionNum-
berOfLine;
    }


  this.lineNumberInPaperOfSectionTitle = function
(paperNumber, sectionNumber)
    {
    if (this.currentPaperNumber != paperNumber)
        {
        this.expandExemplarDataForPaper(paper-
Number)
        }
    return this.sectionArray[sectionNumber].sec-
tionTitleLineNumberInPaper;
    }
  }
//------------------------------------------------/*
```

The languagemap.js Code Library

```
/*
File Name: languagemap.js

--------------------------------------------------

UBDS LanguageMap      last edit 2009-10-25 trb


Copyright (C) 2009 Troy R. Bishop.  All rights
reserved.


LICENSE --------------------------

Permission is hereby granted, free of charge, to
any person obtaining a copy

of this software and associated documentation
files (the "Software"), to deal

in the Software without restriction, including with-
out limitation the rights

to use, copy, modify, merge, publish, distribute,
sublicense, and/or sell

copies of the Software, and to permit persons to
whom the Software is

furnished to do so, subject to the following condi-
tions:


The above copyright notice and this permission
notice shall be included in

all copies or substantial portions of the Software.


THE SOFTWARE IS PROVIDED "AS IS", WITHOUT
WARRANTY OF ANY KIND, EXPRESS OR

IMPLIED, INCLUDING BUT NOT LIMITED TO THE
WARRANTIES OF MERCHANTABILITY,

FITNESS FOR A PARTICULAR PURPOSE AND
NONINFRINGEMENT. IN NO EVENT SHALL THE

AUTHORS OR COPYRIGHT HOLDERS BE LIABLE
```

This object contains the following public methods:

```
textDirection (languageCode)
languageName (languageCode)
scriptName (languageCode)
scriptCode (languageCode)
isValidLanguageCode (languageCode)
languageNameAndCodeArray (fieldForSort)
```

languageCode is a 3-character string from
ISO639-2/T language code register

fieldForSort is a string whose value can be "language code" or "language name"

lineNumber, sectionNumber, and paperNumber
are purely physical and are unmapped.

lineNumber is one-based and unmapped.

sectionNumber is zero-based and unmapped.

paperNumber is zero-based and unmapped.

----

*/

```
//this is the languageMap constructor
function languageMap ()
  {
```

```
//  BEGIN PROPERTIES

   this.vcurrentPaperNumber = null;
   this.vnumberOfSectionsInPaper = null;
   this.vnumberOfLinesInPaper = null;
   this.lineArray = new Array();
   this.sectionArray = new Array();
```

//field names: language code(ISO 639-2/T)^English Language Name^English Script Name^Script Code (ISO 15924)

```
   this.languageAttributesArray =
   {
   "aar" : {"languageName" : "Afar", "scriptName" :
   "Latin", "scriptCode" : "Latn"},

   "abk" : {"languageName" : "Abkhazian", "script-
   Name" : "Cyrillic", "scriptCode" : "Cyrl"},

   "ace" : {"languageName" : "Achinese", "script-
   Name" : "Latin", "scriptCode" : "Latn"},

   "ach" : {"languageName" : "Acoli", "scriptName"
   : "Latin", "scriptCode" : "Latn"},

   "ada" : {"languageName" : "Adangme", "script-
   Name" : "Latin", "scriptCode" : "Latn"},

   "ady" : {"languageName" : "Adyghe", "script-
   Name" : "Cyrillic", "scriptCode" : "Cyri"},

   "afr" : {"languageName" : "Afrikaans", "script-
   Name" : "Latin", "scriptCode" : "Latn"},

   "ain" : {"languageName" : "Ainu", "scriptName" :
   "Latin", "scriptCode" : "Latn"},

   "aka" : {"languageName" : "Akan", "scriptName"
   : "Latin", "scriptCode" : "Latn"},

   "ale" : {"languageName" : "Aleut", "scriptName"
   : "Latin", "scriptCode" : "Latn"},
```

"alt" : {"languageName" : "Southern Altai", "scriptName" : "Cyrillic", "scriptCode" : "Cyrl"},

"amh" : {"languageName" : "Amharic", "scriptName" : "Ethiopic", "scriptCode" : "Ethi"},

"anp" : {"languageName" : "Angika", "scriptName" : "Devanagari", "scriptCode" : "Deva"},

"ara" : {"languageName" : "Arabic", "scriptName" : "Arabic", "scriptCode" : "Arab"},

"arg" : {"languageName" : "Aragonese", "scriptName" : "Latin", "scriptCode" : "Latn"},

"arp" : {"languageName" : "Arapaho", "scriptName" : "Latin", "scriptCode" : "Latn"},

"asm" : {"languageName" : "Assamese", "scriptName" : "Bengali", "scriptCode" : "Beng"},

"ast" : {"languageName" : "Asturian", "scriptName" : "Latin", "scriptCode" : "Latn"},

"ava" : {"languageName" : "Avaric", "scriptName" : "Cyrillic", "scriptCode" : "Cyrl"},

"awa" : {"languageName" : "Awadhi", "scriptName" : "Devanagari", "scriptCode" : "Deva"},

"aym" : {"languageName" : "Aymara", "scriptName" : "Latin", "scriptCode" : "Latn"},

"bak" : {"languageName" : "Bashkir", "scriptName" : "Cyrillic", "scriptCode" : "Cyrl"},

"bam" : {"languageName" : "Bambara", "scriptName" : "Latin", "scriptCode" : "Latn"},

"ban" : {"languageName" : "Balinese", "scriptName" : "Latin", "scriptCode" : "Latn"},

"bas" : {"languageName" : "Basa", "scriptName" : "Latin", "scriptCode" : "Latn"},

"bej" : {"languageName" : "Beja", "scriptName" : "Arabic", "scriptCode" : "Arab"},

"bel" : {"languageName" : "Belarusian", "scriptName" : "Cyrillic", "scriptCode" : "Cyrl"},

"bem" : {"languageName" : "Bemba", "scriptName" : "Latin", "scriptCode" : "Latn"}, "ben" : {"languageName" : "Bengali", "script-Name" : "Bengali", "scriptCode" : "Beng"},

"bho" : {"languageName" : "Bhojpuri", "script-Name" : "Devanagari", "scriptCode" : "Deva"},

"bik" : {"languageName" : "Bikol", "scriptName" : "Latin", "scriptCode" : "Latn"},

"bin" : {"languageName" : "Bin", "scriptName" : "Latin", "scriptCode" : "Latn"},

"bis" : {"languageName" : "Bislama", "script-Name" : "Latin", "scriptCode" : "Latn"},

"bla" : {"languageName" : "Siksika", "script-Name" : "Latin", "scriptCode" : "Latn"},

"bod" : {"languageName" : "Tibetan", "script-Name" : "Tibetan", "scriptCode" : "Tibt"},

"bos" : {"languageName" : "Bosnian", "script-Name" : "Latin", "scriptCode" : "Latn"},

"bra" : {"languageName" : "Braj", "scriptName" : "Devanagari", "scriptCode" : "Deva"},

"bre" : {"languageName" : "Breton", "script-Name" : "Latin", "scriptCode" : "Latn"},

"bua" : {"languageName" : "Buriat", "script-Name" : "Cyrillic", "scriptCode" : "Cyrl"},

"bul" : {"languageName" : "Bulgarian", "script-Name" : "Cyrillic", "scriptCode" : "Cyrl"},

"byn" : {"languageName" : "Blin; Bilin", "script-Name" : "Ethiopic", "scriptCode" : "Ethi"},

"cad" : {"languageName" : "Caddo", "script-Name" : "Latin", "scriptCode" : "Latn"},

"car" : {"languageName" : "Galibi Carib", "script-Name" : "Latin", "scriptCode" : "Latn"},

"cat" : {"languageName" : "Catalan", "script-Name" : "Latin", "scriptCode" : "Latn"},

"ceb" : {"languageName" : "Cebuano", "script-Name" : "Latin", "scriptCode" : "Latn"},

"ces" : {"languageName" : "Czech", "script-Name" : "Latin", "scriptCode" : "Latn"}, "cha" : {"languageName" : "Chamorro", "scriptName" : "Latin", "scriptCode" : "Latn"},

"che" : {"languageName" : "Chechen", "scriptName" : "Cyrillic", "scriptCode" : "Cyrl"},

"chk" : {"languageName" : "Chuukese", "scriptName" : "Latin", "scriptCode" : "Latn"},

"cho" : {"languageName" : "Choctaw", "scriptName" : "Latin", "scriptCode" : "Latn"},

"chp" : {"languageName" : "Chipewyan", "scriptName" : "Latin", "scriptCode" : "Latn"},

"chv" : {"languageName" : "Chuvash", "scriptName" : "Cyrillic", "scriptCode" : "Cyrl"},

"chy" : {"languageName" : "Cheyenne", "scriptName" : "Latin", "scriptCode" : "Latn"},

"cor" : {"languageName" : "Cornish", "scriptName" : "Latin", "scriptCode" : "Latn"},

"cos" : {"languageName" : "Corsican", "scriptName" : "Latin", "scriptCode" : "Latn"},

"crh" : {"languageName" : "Crimean Turkish", "scriptName" : "Cyrillic", "scriptCode" : "Cyrl"},

"cym" : {"languageName" : "Welsh", "scriptName" : "Latin", "scriptCode" : "Latn"},

"dak" : {"languageName" : "Dakota", "scriptName" : "Latin", "scriptCode" : "Latn"},

"dan" : {"languageName" : "Danish", "scriptName" : "Latin", "scriptCode" : "Latn"},

"dar" : {"languageName" : "Dargwa", "scriptName" : "Cyrillic", "scriptCode" : "Cyrl"},

"del" : {"languageName" : "Delaware", "scriptName" : "Latin", "scriptCode" : "Latn"},

"den" : {"languageName" : "Slave", "scriptName" : "Latin", "scriptCode" : "Latn"},

"deu" : {"languageName" : "German", "scriptName" : "Latin", "scriptCode" : "Latn"},

"dgr" : {"languageName" : "Dogrib", "scriptName" : "Latin", "scriptCode" : "Latn"}, "din" : {"languageName" : "Dinka", "scriptName" : "Latin", "scriptCode" : "Latn"},

"div" : {"languageName" : "Diveh", "scriptName" : "Thaana", "scriptCode" : "Thaa"},

"doi" : {"languageName" : "Dogri", "scriptName" : "Arabic", "scriptCode" : "Arab"},

"dsb" : {"languageName" : "Lower Sorbian", "scriptName" : "Latin", "scriptCode" : "Latn"},

"dua" : {"languageName" : "Duala", "scriptName" : "Latin", "scriptCode" : "Latn"},

"dyu" : {"languageName" : "Dyula", "scriptName" : "Latin", "scriptCode" : "Latn"},

"dzo" : {"languageName" : "Dzongkha", "scriptName" : "Tibetan", "scriptCode" : "Tibt"},

"efi" : {"languageName" : "Efik", "scriptName" : "Latin", "scriptCode" : "Latn"},

"eka" : {"languageName" : "Ekajuk", "scriptName" : "Latin", "scriptCode" : "Latn"},

"ell" : {"languageName" : "Greek, Modern (1453-)", "scriptName" : "Greek", "scriptCode" : "Grek"},

"eng" : {"languageName" : "English", "scriptName" : "Latin", "scriptCode" : "Latn"},

"est" : {"languageName" : "Estonian", "scriptName" : "Latin", "scriptCode" : "Latn"},

"eus" : {"languageName" : "Basque", "scriptName" : "Latin", "scriptCode" : "Latn"},

"ewe" : {"languageName" : "Ewe", "scriptName" : "Latin", "scriptCode" : "Latn"},

"ewo" : {"languageName" : "Ewondo", "scriptName" : "Latin", "scriptCode" : "Latn"},

"fan" : {"languageName" : "Fang", "scriptName" : "Latin", "scriptCode" : "Latn"},

"fao" : {"languageName" : "Faroese", "scriptName" : "Latin", "scriptCode" : "Latn"},

"fas" : {"languageName" : "Persian", "scriptName" : "Arabic", "scriptCode" : "Arab"}, "fat" : {"languageName" : "Fanti", "scriptName" : "Latin", "scriptCode" : "Latn"},

"fij" : {"languageName" : "Fijian", "scriptName" : "Latin", "scriptCode" : "Latn"},

"fil" : {"languageName" : "Filipino", "scriptName" : "Latin", "scriptCode" : "Latn"},

"fin" : {"languageName" : "Finnish", "scriptName" : "Latin", "scriptCode" : "Latn"},

"fon" : {"languageName" : "Fon", "scriptName" : "Latin", "scriptCode" : "Latn"},

"fra" : {"languageName" : "French", "scriptName" : "Latin", "scriptCode" : "Latn"},

"frr" : {"languageName" : "Northern Frisian", "scriptName" : "Latin", "scriptCode" : "Latn"},

"frs" : {"languageName" : "Eastern Frisian", "scriptName" : "Latin", "scriptCode" : "Latn"},

"fry" : {"languageName" : "Western Frisian", "scriptName" : "Latin", "scriptCode" : "Latn"},

"ful" : {"languageName" : "Fulah", "scriptName" : "Latin", "scriptCode" : "Latn"},

"fur" : {"languageName" : "Friulian", "scriptName" : "Latin", "scriptCode" : "Latn"},

"gaa" : {"languageName" : "Ga", "scriptName" : "Latin", "scriptCode" : "Latn"},

"gay" : {"languageName" : "Gayo", "scriptName" : "Arabic", "scriptCode" : "Arab"},

"gba" : {"languageName" : "Gbaya", "scriptName" : "Arabic", "scriptCode" : "Arab"},

"gil" : {"languageName" : "Gilbertese", "scriptName" : "Latin", "scriptCode" : "Latn"},

"gle" : {"languageName" : "Irish", "scriptName" : "Latin", "scriptCode" : "Latn"},

"glg" : {"languageName" : "Galician", "scriptName" : "Latin", "scriptCode" : "Latn"},

"glv" : {"languageName" : "Manx", "scriptName" : "Latin", "scriptCode" : "Latn"}, "gor" : {"languageName" : "Gorontalo", "scriptName" : "Latin", "scriptCode" : "Latn"},

"grb" : {"languageName" : "Grebo", "scriptName" : "Latin", "scriptCode" : "Latn"},

"grn" : {"languageName" : "Guarani", "scriptName" : "Latin", "scriptCode" : "Latn"},

"gsw" : {"languageName" : "Swiss German", "scriptName" : "Latin", "scriptCode" : "Latn"},

"guj" : {"languageName" : "Gujarati", "scriptName" : "Gujarati", "scriptCode" : "Gujr"},

"gwi" : {"languageName" : "Gwich'in", "scriptName" : "Latin", "scriptCode" : "Latn"},

"hai" : {"languageName" : "Haida", "scriptName" : "Latin", "scriptCode" : "Latn"},

"hat" : {"languageName" : "Haitian", "scriptName" : "Latin", "scriptCode" : "Latn"},

"haw" : {"languageName" : "Hawaiian", "scriptName" : "Latin", "scriptCode" : "Latn"},

"heb" : {"languageName" : "Hebrew", "scriptName" : "Hebrew", "scriptCode" : "Hebr"},

"her" : {"languageName" : "Herero", "scriptName" : "Latin", "scriptCode" : "Latn"},

"hil" : {"languageName" : "Hiligaynon", "scriptName" : "Latin", "scriptCode" : "Latn"},

"hin" : {"languageName" : "Hindi", "scriptName" : "Devanagari", "scriptCode" : "Deva"},

"hmn" : {"languageName" : "Hmong", "scriptName" : "Latin", "scriptCode" : "Latn"},

"hmo" : {"languageName" : "Hiri Motu", "scriptName" : "Latin", "scriptCode" : "Latn"},

"hrv" : {"languageName" : "Croatian", "scriptName" : "Latin", "scriptCode" : "Latn"},

"hsb" : {"languageName" : "Upper Sorbian", "scriptName" : "Latin", "scriptCode" : "Latn"},

"hun" : {"languageName" : "Hungarian", "scriptName" : "Latin", "scriptCode" : "Latn"}, "hup" : {"languageName" : "Hupa", "scriptName" : "Latin", "scriptCode" : "Latn"},

"hye" : {"languageName" : "Armenian", "scriptName" : "Armenian", "scriptCode" : "Armn"},

"iba" : {"languageName" : "Iban", "scriptName" : "Latin", "scriptCode" : "Latn"},

"ibo" : {"languageName" : "Igbo", "scriptName" : "Latin", "scriptCode" : "Latn"},

"iii" : {"languageName" : "Sichuan Yi", "scriptName" : "Yi", "scriptCode" : "Yiii"},

"ilo" : {"languageName" : "Iloko", "scriptName" : "Latin", "scriptCode" : "Latn"},

"ind" : {"languageName" : "Indonesian", "scriptName" : "Latin", "scriptCode" : "Latn"},

"inh" : {"languageName" : "Ingush", "scriptName" : "Cyrillic", "scriptCode" : "Cyrl"},

"ipk" : {"languageName" : "Inupiaq", "scriptName" : "Latin", "scriptCode" : "Latn"},

"isl" : {"languageName" : "Icelandic", "scriptName" : "Latin", "scriptCode" : "Latn"},

"ita" : {"languageName" : "Italian", "scriptName" : "Latin", "scriptCode" : "Latn"},

"jav" : {"languageName" : "Javanese", "scriptName" : "Latin", "scriptCode" : "Latn"},

"jpn" : {"languageName" : "Japanese", "scriptName" : "Japanese", "scriptCode" : "Jpan"},

"jpr" : {"languageName" : "Judeo-Persian", "scriptName" : "Hebrew", "scriptCode" : "Hebr"},

"jrb" : {"languageName" : "Judeo-Arabic", "scriptName" : "Hebrew", "scriptCode" : "Hebr"},

"kaa" : {"languageName" : "Kara-Kalpak", "scriptName" : "Cyrillic", "scriptCode" : "Cyrl"},

"kab" : {"languageName" : "Kabyle", "scriptName" : "Latin", "scriptCode" : "Latn"},

"kac" : {"languageName" : "Kachin", "scriptName" : "Myanmar", "scriptCode" : "Mymr"}, "kal" : {"languageName" : "Kalaallisut", "script-Name" : "Latin", "scriptCode" : "Latn"},

"kam" : {"languageName" : "Kamba", "script-Name" : "Latin", "scriptCode" : "Latn"},

"kan" : {"languageName" : "Kannada", "script-Name" : "Kannada", "scriptCode" : "Knda"},

"kat" : {"languageName" : "Georgian", "script-Name" : "Georgian", "scriptCode" : "Geor"},

"kau" : {"languageName" : "Kanuri", "script-Name" : "Latin", "scriptCode" : "Latn"},

"kaz" : {"languageName" : "Kazakh", "script-Name" : "Cyrillic", "scriptCode" : "Cyrl"},

"kbd" : {"languageName" : "Kabardian", "script-Name" : "Cyrillic", "scriptCode" : "Cyrl"},

"kha" : {"languageName" : "Khasi", "script-Name" : "Latin", "scriptCode" : "Latn"},

"khm" : {"languageName" : "Central Khmer", "scriptName" : "Khmer", "scriptCode" : "Khmr"},

"kik" : {"languageName" : "Kikuyu", "script-Name" : "Latin", "scriptCode" : "Latn"},

"kin" : {"languageName" : "Kinyarwanda", "scriptName" : "Latin", "scriptCode" : "Latn"},

"kmb" : {"languageName" : "Kimbundu", "script-Name" : "Latin", "scriptCode" : "Latn"},

"kok" : {"languageName" : "Konkani", "script-Name" : "Devanagari", "scriptCode" : "Deva"},

"kon" : {"languageName" : "Kongo", "script-Name" : "Latin", "scriptCode" : "Latn"},

"kor" : {"languageName" : "Korean", "script-Name" : "Korean", "scriptCode" : "Kore"},

"kos" : {"languageName" : "Kosraean", "script-Name" : "Latin", "scriptCode" : "Latn"},

"kpe" : {"languageName" : "Kpelle", "script-Name" : "Latin", "scriptCode" : "Latn"},

"krc" : {"languageName" : "Karachay-Balkar", "scriptName" : "Cyrillic", "scriptCode" : "Cyrl"}, "kru" : {"languageName" : "Kurukh", "scriptName" : "Devanagari", "scriptCode" : "Deva"},

"kua" : {"languageName" : "Kuanyama", "scriptName" : "Latin", "scriptCode" : "Latn"},

"kum" : {"languageName" : "Kumyk", "scriptName" : "Cyrillic", "scriptCode" : "Cyrl"},

"kut" : {"languageName" : "Kutenai", "scriptName" : "Latin", "scriptCode" : "Latn"},

"lad" : {"languageName" : "Ladino", "scriptName" : "Hebrew", "scriptCode" : "Hebr"},

"lah" : {"languageName" : "Lahnda", "scriptName" : "Arabic", "scriptCode" : "Arab"},

"lao" : {"languageName" : "Lao", "scriptName" : "Lao", "scriptCode" : "Laoo"},

"lav" : {"languageName" : "Latvian", "scriptName" : "Latin", "scriptCode" : "Latn"},

"lez" : {"languageName" : "Lezghian", "scriptName" : "Cyrillic", "scriptCode" : "Cyrl"},

"lim" : {"languageName" : "Limburgish", "scriptName" : "Latin", "scriptCode" : "Latn"},

"lin" : {"languageName" : "Lingala", "scriptName" : "Latin", "scriptCode" : "Latn"},

"lit" : {"languageName" : "Lithuanian", "scriptName" : "Latin", "scriptCode" : "Latn"},

"lol" : {"languageName" : "Mongo", "scriptName" : "Latin", "scriptCode" : "Latn"},

"loz" : {"languageName" : "Lozi", "scriptName" : "Latin", "scriptCode" : "Latn"},

"ltz" : {"languageName" : "Luxembourgish", "scriptName" : "Latin", "scriptCode" : "Latn"},

"lua" : {"languageName" : "Luba-Lulua", "scriptName" : "Latin", "scriptCode" : "Latn"},

"lub" : {"languageName" : "Luba-Katanga", "scriptName" : "Latin", "scriptCode" : "Latn"}, "lug" : {"languageName" : "Ganda", "script-Name" : "Latin", "scriptCode" : "Latn"},

"lui" : {"languageName" : "Luiseno", "script-Name" : "Latin", "scriptCode" : "Latn"},

"lun" : {"languageName" : "Lunda", "script-Name" : "Latin", "scriptCode" : "Latn"},

"luo" : {"languageName" : "Luo (Kenya and Tanzania)", "scriptName" : "Latin", "scriptCode" : "Latn"},

"lus" : {"languageName" : "Lushai", "script-Name" : "Bengali", "scriptCode" : "Beng"},

"mad" : {"languageName" : "Madurese", "script-Name" : "Latin", "scriptCode" : "Latn"},

"mag" : {"languageName" : "Magahi", "script-Name" : "Devanagari", "scriptCode" : "Deva"},

"mah" : {"languageName" : "Marshallese", "scriptName" : "Latin", "scriptCode" : "Latn"},

"mai" : {"languageName" : "Maithili", "script-Name" : "Devanagari", "scriptCode" : "Deva"},

"mak" : {"languageName" : "Makasar", "script-Name" : "Latin", "scriptCode" : "Latn"},

"mal" : {"languageName" : "Malayalam", "script-Name" : "Malayalam", "scriptCode" : "Mlym"},

"man" : {"languageName" : "Mandingo", "script-Name" : "Latin", "scriptCode" : "Latn"},

"mar" : {"languageName" : "Marathi", "script-Name" : "Devanagari", "scriptCode" : "Deva"},

"mas" : {"languageName" : "Masai", "script-Name" : "Latin", "scriptCode" : "Latn"},

"mdf" : {"languageName" : "Moksha", "script-Name" : "Cyrillic", "scriptCode" : "Cyrl"},

"mdr" : {"languageName" : "Mandar", "script-Name" : "Latin", "scriptCode" : "Latn"},

"men" : {"languageName" : "Mende", "script-Name" : "Latin", "scriptCode" : "Latn"},

"mic" : {"languageName" : "Micmac", "script-

Name" : "Latin", "scriptCode" : "Latn"},

"min" : {"languageName" : "Minangkabau", "scriptName" : "Latin", "scriptCode" : "Latn"},

"mkd" : {"languageName" : "Macedonian", "scriptName" : "Cyrillic", "scriptCode" : "Cyrl"},

"mlg" : {"languageName" : "Malagasy", "scriptName" : "Latin", "scriptCode" : "Latn"},

"mlt" : {"languageName" : "Maltese", "scriptName" : "Latin", "scriptCode" : "Latn"},

"mni" : {"languageName" : "Manipuri", "scriptName" : "Bengali", "scriptCode" : "Beng"},

"moh" : {"languageName" : "Mohawk", "scriptName" : "Latin", "scriptCode" : "Latn"},

"mos" : {"languageName" : "Mossi", "scriptName" : "Latin", "scriptCode" : "Latn"},

"mri" : {"languageName" : "Maori", "scriptName" : "Latin", "scriptCode" : "Latn"},

"msa" : {"languageName" : "Malay", "scriptName" : "Latin", "scriptCode" : "Latn"},

"mus" : {"languageName" : "Creek", "scriptName" : "Latin", "scriptCode" : "Latn"},

"mwl" : {"languageName" : "Mirandese", "scriptName" : "Latin", "scriptCode" : "Latn"},

"mwr" : {"languageName" : "Marwari", "scriptName" : "Devanagari", "scriptCode" : "Deva"},

"mya" : {"languageName" : "Burmese", "scriptName" : "Myanmar", "scriptCode" : "Mymr"},

"myv" : {"languageName" : "Erzya", "scriptName" : "Cyrillic", "scriptCode" : "Cyrl"},

"nap" : {"languageName" : "Neapolitan", "scriptName" : "Latin", "scriptCode" : "Latn"},

"nau" : {"languageName" : "Nauru", "scriptName" : "Latin", "scriptCode" : "Latn"},

"nav" : {"languageName" : "Navajoo", "scriptName" : "Latin", "scriptCode" : "Latn"}, "ndo" : {"languageName" : "Ndonga", "script-Name" : "Latin", "scriptCode" : "Latn"},

"nds" : {"languageName" : "Low German", "scriptName" : "Latin", "scriptCode" : "Latn"},

"nep" : {"languageName" : "Nepali", "script-Name" : "Devanagari", "scriptCode" : "Deva"},

"new" : {"languageName" : "Newari", "script-Name" : "Devanagari", "scriptCode" : "Deva"},

"nia" : {"languageName" : "Nias", "scriptName" : "Latin", "scriptCode" : "Latn"},

"niu" : {"languageName" : "Niuean", "script-Name" : "Latin", "scriptCode" : "Latn"},

"nld" : {"languageName" : "Dutch", "scriptName" : "Latin", "scriptCode" : "Latn"},

"nno" : {"languageName" : "Norwegian Nynorsk", "scriptName" : "Latin", "scriptCode" : "Latn"},

"nog" : {"languageName" : "Nogai", "script-Name" : "Cyrillic", "scriptCode" : "Cyrl"},

"nor" : {"languageName" : "Norwegian", "script-Name" : "Latin", "scriptCode" : "Latn"},

"nqo" : {"languageName" : "N'Ko", "scriptName" : "N'Ko", "scriptCode" : "Nkoo"},

"nso" : {"languageName" : "Northern Sotho", "scriptName" : "Latin", "scriptCode" : "Latn"},

"nya" : {"languageName" : "Nyanja", "script-Name" : "Latin", "scriptCode" : "Latn"},

"nym" : {"languageName" : "Nyamwezi", "script-Name" : "Latin", "scriptCode" : "Latn"},

"nyn" : {"languageName" : "Nyankole", "script-Name" : "Latin", "scriptCode" : "Latn"},

"nyo" : {"languageName" : "Nyoro", "script-Name" : "Latin", "scriptCode" : "Latn"},

"nzi" : {"languageName" : "Nzima", "scriptName" : "Latin", "scriptCode" : "Latn"},

"oci" : {"languageName" : "Occitan (post 1500)",

"scriptName" : "Latin", "scriptCode" : "Latn"},

  "ori" : {"languageName" : "Oriya", "scriptName" : "Oriya", "scriptCode" : "Orya"},

  "orm" : {"languageName" : "Oromo", "scriptName" : "Latin", "scriptCode" : "Latn"},

  "osa" : {"languageName" : "Osage", "scriptName" : "Latin", "scriptCode" : "Latn"},

  "pag" : {"languageName" : "Pangasinan", "scriptName" : "Latin", "scriptCode" : "Latn"},

  "pam" : {"languageName" : "Pampanga", "scriptName" : "Latin", "scriptCode" : "Latn"},

  "pan" : {"languageName" : "Punjabi", "scriptName" : "Gurmukhi", "scriptCode" : "Guru"},

  "pap" : {"languageName" : "Papiamento", "scriptName" : "Latin", "scriptCode" : "Latn"},

  "pau" : {"languageName" : "Palauan", "scriptName" : "Latin", "scriptCode" : "Latn"},

  "pol" : {"languageName" : "Polish", "scriptName" : "Latin", "scriptCode" : "Latn"},

  "pon" : {"languageName" : "Pohnpeian", "scriptName" : "Latin", "scriptCode" : "Latn"},

  "por" : {"languageName" : "Portuguese", "scriptName" : "Latin", "scriptCode" : "Latn"},

  "pus" : {"languageName" : "Pashto", "scriptName" : "Arabic", "scriptCode" : "Arab"},

  "que" : {"languageName" : "Quechua", "scriptName" : "Latin", "scriptCode" : "Latn"},

  "raj" : {"languageName" : "Rajasthani", "scriptName" : "Latin", "scriptCode" : "Latn"},

  "rap" : {"languageName" : "Rapanui", "scriptName" : "Latin", "scriptCode" : "Latn"},

  "rar" : {"languageName" : "Rarotongan", "scriptName" : "Latin", "scriptCode" : "Latn"},

  "ron" : {"languageName" : "Romanian", "scriptName" : "Latin", "scriptCode" : "Latn"},

```
    "run" : {"languageName" : "Rundi", "script-
Name" : "Latin", "scriptCode" : "Latn"},

    "rup" : {"languageName" : "Aromanian", "script-
Name" : "Latin", "scriptCode" : "Latn"},

    "rus" : {"languageName" : "Russian", "script-
Name" : "Cyrillic", "scriptCode" : "Cyrl"},

    "sad" : {"languageName" : "Sandawe", "script-
Name" : "Latin", "scriptCode" : "Latn"},

    "sag" : {"languageName" : "Sango", "script-
Name" : "Latin", "scriptCode" : "Latn"},

    "sah" : {"languageName" : "Yakut", "scriptName"
: "Cyrillic", "scriptCode" : "Cyrl"},

    "sas" : {"languageName" : "Sasak", "script-
Name" : "Latin", "scriptCode" : "Latn"},

    "sat" : {"languageName" : "Santali", "script-
Name" : "Latin", "scriptCode" : "Latn"},

    "scn" : {"languageName" : "Sicilian", "script-
Name" : "Latin", "scriptCode" : "Latn"},

    "sco" : {"languageName" : "Scots", "script-
Name" : "Latin", "scriptCode" : "Latn"},

    "shn" : {"languageName" : "Shan", "scriptName"
: "Myanmar", "scriptCode" : "Mymr"},

    "sid" : {"languageName" : "Sidamo", "script-
Name" : "Latin", "scriptCode" : "Latn"},

    "sin" : {"languageName" : "Sinhala", "script-
Name" : "Sinhala", "scriptCode" : "Sinh"},

    "slk" : {"languageName" : "Slovak", "script-
Name" : "Latin", "scriptCode" : "Latn"},

    "slv" : {"languageName" : "Slovenian", "script-
Name" : "Latin", "scriptCode" : "Latn"},

    "sma" : {"languageName" : "Southern Sami",
"scriptName" : "Latin", "scriptCode" : "Latn"},

    "sme" : {"languageName" : "Northern Sami",
"scriptName" : "Latin", "scriptCode" : "Latn"},

    "smj" : {"languageName" : "Lule Sami", "script-
Name" : "Latin", "scriptCode" : "Latn"},
```

"smn" : {"languageName" : "Inari Sami", "script-Name" : "Latin", "scriptCode" : "Latn"},

"smo" : {"languageName" : "Samoan", "script-Name" : "Latin", "scriptCode" : "Latn"},

"sms" : {"languageName" : "Skolt Sami", "script-Name" : "Latin", "scriptCode" : "Latn"},

"sna" : {"languageName" : "Shona", "script-Name" : "Latin", "scriptCode" : "Latn"},

"snk" : {"languageName" : "Soninke", "script-Name" : "Latin", "scriptCode" : "Latn"},

"som" : {"languageName" : "Somali", "script-Name" : "Latin", "scriptCode" : "Latn"},

"sot" : {"languageName" : "Sotho, Southern", "scriptName" : "Latin", "scriptCode" : "Latn"},

"spa" : {"languageName" : "Spanish", "script-Name" : "Latin", "scriptCode" : "Latn"},

"sqi" : {"languageName" : "Albanian", "script-Name" : "Latin", "scriptCode" : "Latn"},

"srd" : {"languageName" : "Sardinian", "script-Name" : "Latin", "scriptCode" : "Latn"},

"srn" : {"languageName" : "Sranan Tongo", "scriptName" : "Latin", "scriptCode" : "Latn"},

"srr" : {"languageName" : "Serer", "scriptName" : "Latin", "scriptCode" : "Latn"},

"ssw" : {"languageName" : "Swati", "script-Name" : "Latin", "scriptCode" : "Latn"},

"suk" : {"languageName" : "Sukuma", "script-Name" : "Latin", "scriptCode" : "Latn"},

"sun" : {"languageName" : "Sundanese", "script-Name" : "Latin", "scriptCode" : "Latn"},

"sus" : {"languageName" : "Susu", "scriptName" : "Latin", "scriptCode" : "Latn"},

"swa" : {"languageName" : "Swahili", "script-Name" : "Latin", "scriptCode" : "Latn"},

"swe" : {"languageName" : "Swedish", "script-Name" : "Latin", "scriptCode" : "Latn"},

```
"tah" : {"languageName" : "Tahitian", "script-
Name" : "Latin", "scriptCode" : "Latn"},

    "tam" : {"languageName" : "Tamil", "scriptName"
: "Tamil", "scriptCode" : "Taml"},

    "tat" : {"languageName" : "Tatar", "scriptName" :
"Cyrillic", "scriptCode" : "Cyrl"},

    "tel" : {"languageName" : "Telugu", "scriptName"
: "Telugu", "scriptCode" : "Telu"},

    "tem" : {"languageName" : "Timne", "script-
Name" : "Latin", "scriptCode" : "Latn"},

    "ter" : {"languageName" : "Tereno", "script-
Name" : "Latin", "scriptCode" : "Latn"},

    "tet" : {"languageName" : "Tetum", "scriptName"
: "Latin", "scriptCode" : "Latn"},

    "tgl" : {"languageName" : "Tagalog", "script-
Name" : "Latin", "scriptCode" : "Latn"},

    "tha" : {"languageName" : "Thai", "scriptName" :
"Thai", "scriptCode" : "Thai"},

    "tig" : {"languageName" : "Tigre", "scriptName" :
"Ethiopic", "scriptCode" : "Ethi"},

    "tir" : {"languageName" : "Tigrinya", "script-
Name" : "Ethiopic", "scriptCode" : "Ethi"},

    "tiv" : {"languageName" : "Tiv", "scriptName" :
"Latin", "scriptCode" : "Latn"},

    "tkl" : {"languageName" : "Tokelau", "script-
Name" : "Latin", "scriptCode" : "Latn"},

    "tli" : {"languageName" : "Tlingit", "scriptName"
: "Latin", "scriptCode" : "Latn"},

    "tmh" : {"languageName" : "Tamashek", "script-
Name" : "Latin", "scriptCode" : "Latn"},

    "tog" : {"languageName" : "Tonga (Nyasa)",
"scriptName" : "Latin", "scriptCode" : "Latn"},

    "ton" : {"languageName" : "Tonga (Tonga
Islands)", "scriptName" : "Latin", "scriptCode" :
"Latn"},

    "tpi" : {"languageName" : "Tok Pisin", "script-
```

Name" : "Latin", "scriptCode" : "Latn"},

"tsi" : {"languageName" : "Tsimshian", "script-
Name" : "Latin", "scriptCode" : "Latn"},

"tsn" : {"languageName" : "Tswana", "script-
Name" : "Latin", "scriptCode" : "Latn"},

"tso" : {"languageName" : "Tsonga", "script-
Name" : "Latin", "scriptCode" : "Latn"},

"tum" : {"languageName" : "Tumbuka", "script-
Name" : "Latin", "scriptCode" : "Latn"},

"tur" : {"languageName" : "Turkish", "script-
Name" : "Latin", "scriptCode" : "Latn"},

"tvl" : {"languageName" : "Tuvalu", "scriptName"
: "Latin", "scriptCode" : "Latn"},

"twi" : {"languageName" : "Twi", "scriptName" :
"Latin", "scriptCode" : "Latn"},

"tyv" : {"languageName" : "Tuvinian", "script-
Name" : "Cyrillic", "scriptCode" : "Cyrl"},

"udm" : {"languageName" : "Udmurt", "script-
Name" : "Cyrillic", "scriptCode" : "Cyrl"},

"uig" : {"languageName" : "Uighur", "script-
Name" : "Arabic", "scriptCode" : "Arab"},

"ukr" : {"languageName" : "Ukrainian", "script-
Name" : "Cyrillic", "scriptCode" : "Cyrl"},

"umb" : {"languageName" : "Umbundu", "script-
Name" : "Latin", "scriptCode" : "Latn"},

"urd" : {"languageName" : "Urdu", "scriptName"
: "Arabic", "scriptCode" : "Arab"},

"vai" : {"languageName" : "Vai", "scriptName" :
"Vai", "scriptCode" : "Vaii"},

"ven" : {"languageName" : "Venda", "script-
Name" : "Latin", "scriptCode" : "Latn"},

"vie" : {"languageName" : "Vietnamese", "script-
Name" : "Latin", "scriptCode" : "Latn"},

"war" : {"languageName" : "Waray", "script-
Name" : "Latin", "scriptCode" : "Latn"},

```
        "was" : {"languageName" : "Washo", "script-
Name" : "Latin", "scriptCode" : "Latn"},

        "wln" : {"languageName" : "Walloon", "script-
Name" : "Latin", "scriptCode" : "Latn"},

        "wol" : {"languageName" : "Wolof", "script-
Name" : "Latin", "scriptCode" : "Latn"},

        "xal" : {"languageName" : "Kalmyk", "script-
Name" : "Cyrillic", "scriptCode" : "Cyrl"},

        "xho" : {"languageName" : "Xhosa", "script-
Name" : "Latin", "scriptCode" : "Latn"},

        "yao" : {"languageName" : "Yao", "scriptName" :
"Latin", "scriptCode" : "Latn"},

        "yap" : {"languageName" : "Yapese", "script-
Name" : "Latin", "scriptCode" : "Latn"},

        "yid" : {"languageName" : "Yiddish", "script-
Name" : "Hebrew", "scriptCode" : "Hebr"},

        "yor" : {"languageName" : "Yoruba", "script-
Name" : "Latin", "scriptCode" : "Latn"},

        "zap" : {"languageName" : "Zapotec", "script-
Name" : "Latin", "scriptCode" : "Latn"},

        "zha" : {"languageName" : "Zhuang", "script-
Name" : "Latin", "scriptCode" : "Latn"},

        "zul" : {"languageName" : "Zulu", "scriptName" :
"Latin", "scriptCode" : "Latn"},

        "zun" : {"languageName" : "Zuni", "scriptName"
: "Latin", "scriptCode" : "Latn"},

        "zza" : {"languageName" : "Zaza", "scriptName" :
"Arabic", "scriptCode" : "Arab"}
    };
//----------------------------------------------

//   END PROPERTIES


//   BEGIN METHODS
```

```
this.textDirection = function (languageCode)
    {
    if (this.languageAttributesArray[language-
Code].scriptCode === undefined)
        {
        return false;
        }
    var scriptCode = this.languageAttributesAr-
ray[languageCode].scriptCode;
    // Arabic, Hebrew, and Thaana are the only rtl
scripts today
    if (scriptCode == "Arab" || scriptCode ==
"Hebr" || scriptCode == "Thaa")
        {
        return "rtl";
        }
    else
        {
        return "ltr";
        }
    }


this.languageName = function (languageCode)
    {
    if (this.languageAttributesArray[language-
Code].languageName === undefined)
        {
        return false;
        }
    return this.languageAttributesArray[language-
Code].languageName;
    }
```

```
this.scriptName = function (languageCode)
{
if (this.languageAttributesArray[language-
Code].scriptName === undefined)
{
return false;
}
return this.languageAttributesArray[language-
Code].scriptName;
}


this.scriptCode = function (languageCode)
{
if (this.languageAttributesArray[language-
Code].scriptCode === undefined)
{
return false;
}
return this.languageAttributesArray[language-
Code].scriptCode;
}


this.isValidLanguageCode = function (language-
Code)
{
if (this.languageAttributesArray[languageCode]
=== undefined)
{
return false;
}
else
```

```
        {
        return true;
        }
    }


    this.languageNameAndCodeArray = function
(fieldForSort)
        {
        var arrayForReturn = new Array();
        var languageKeyArray = new Array();
        var displayString = "";
        var workArray = new Array();
        var newKey = null;
        var newArgument = null;
        var consolidateKey = null;


        if (fieldForSort == "languageCode")
            {
            for (var createIndex in this.languageAttribute-
sArray)
                {
                workArray[createIndex] = this.languageAt-
tributesArray[createIndex].languageName;
                languageKeyArray[languageKeyArray.
length] = createIndex;
                }
            }
        else if (fieldForSort == "languageName")
            {
            for (var createIndex in this.languageAttribute-
sArray)
                {
```

```
            newKey = this.languageAttributesArray[cre-
ateIndex].languageName;
        workArray[newKey] = createIndex;
        languageKeyArray[languageKeyArray.
length] = newKey;
            }
        }
    else
        {
        return 0;
        }
    languageKeyArray.sort();


    for (consolidateIndex = 0; consolidateIndex <
languageKeyArray.length; consolidateIndex++)
        {
        consolidateKey = languageKeyArray[consoli-
dateIndex];
        arrayForReturn[consolidateIndex] = new
Array();
        arrayForReturn[consolidateIndex][0] = con-
solidateKey;
        arrayForReturn[consolidateIndex][1] = work-
Array[consolidateKey];
        }
    return arrayForReturn;
    }
  }
//-------------------------------------------------
```

The ubt_analyzer.js Code Library

```
/*

File Name: ubt_analyzer.js

----------------------------------------

Urantia Book Translator


Copyright (C) 2007, 2009 Troy R. Bishop.  All rights
reserved.


Module ubt_analyzer.js     last edit 20009-08-21 trb


LICENSE ------------------------
Permission is hereby granted, free of charge, to
any person obtaining a copy

of this software and associated documentation
files (the "Software"), to deal

in the Software without restriction, including with-
out limitation the rights

to use, copy, modify, merge, publish, distribute,
sublicense, and/or sell

copies of the Software, and to permit persons to
whom the Software is

furnished to do so, subject to the following condi-
tions:


The above copyright notice and this permission
notice shall be included in

all copies or substantial portions of the Software.


THE SOFTWARE IS PROVIDED "AS IS", WITHOUT
WARRANTY OF ANY KIND, EXPRESS OR

IMPLIED, INCLUDING BUT NOT LIMITED TO THE
WARRANTIES OF MERCHANTABILITY,
```

FITNESS FOR A PARTICULAR PURPOSE AND NONINFRINGEMENT. IN NO EVENT SHALL THE

AUTHORS OR COPYRIGHT HOLDERS BE LIABLE FOR ANY CLAIM, DAMAGES OR OTHER

LIABILITY, WHETHER IN AN ACTION OF CON-TRACT, TORT OR OTHERWISE, ARISING FROM,

OUT OF OR IN CONNECTION WITH THE SOFT-WARE OR THE USE OR OTHER DEALINGS IN

THE SOFTWARE.

```
*/

//----------Begin Functions-------------


//-------------------------------------
// function getLaLanguageCodenguageCodeList
(languageCategory)
//-------------------------------------
function getLanguageCodeList (languageCatego-
ry)
  {
  var fso = new ActiveXObject("Scripting.FileSys-
temObject");
  var categoryFolder = fso.GetFolder("./" + lan-
guageCategory);
  var categorySubfoldersCollection = new Array();
  var categorySubfolders = new Enumerator(cate-
goryFolder.SubFolders);


  for (; !categorySubfolders.atEnd(); categorySub-
folders.moveNext())
    {
    categorySubfoldersCollection[categorySub-
foldersCollection.length] = categorySubfolders.
item().name;
    }
```

```
    return categorySubfoldersCollection;
    }


//----------------------------------------------------------
// function fileName (paperNumber)
//----------------------------------------------------------
function fileName (paperNumber)
  {
  return filePath + languageCode + "_" + paper-
Type + "_p" + zeroedPaperNumber(paperNumber)
+ ".u16";
  }


//----------------------------------------------------------
// function analyzerNumberOfSublinesInLine ()
//----------------------------------------------------------
function analyzerNumberOfSublinesInLine ()
  {
  var sublinesKey = currentAnalyzerPaperNumber
+ ":" + analyzerInputLineNumber;
  for (var sublinesNumber in sublinesInLineArray)
    {
    if (sublinesNumber == sublinesKey)
      {
      return sublinesInLineArray[sublinesKey];
      }
    }
  return 0;
  }


//----------------------------------------------------------
```

```
// function analyzerFileExists (paperNumber)
//-------------------------------------------------------
function analyzerFileExists (paperNumber)
   {
   var fso, f, s;
   fso = new ActiveXObject("Scripting.FileSystem-
Object");
   return fso.FileExists(fileName(paperNumber));
   }


/*
//-------------------------------------------------------
// function hideWaitBar ()
//-------------------------------------------------------
function hideWaitBar ()
   {
   waitObj.style.display = "none";
   }


//-------------------------------------------------------
// function showWaitBar ()
//-------------------------------------------------------
function showWaitBar ()
   {
//   waitObj.style.top = "60 px";
//   var newWidth = (screen.availWidth / 2) - 81;
//   newWidth = newWidth + "px";
//   waitObj.style.left = newWidth;
   waitObj.style.display = "";
//   waitObj.style.zIndex = 2000;
```

```
     }
*/


//----------------------------------------------------------
// function createBlankFileAttributesArray ()
//----------------------------------------------------------
function createBlankFileAttributesArray ()
   {
   var fileIndex = null;
   var attributesFile = null;
   analyzerFileAttributesObjArray = [];

   for (fileIndex = 0; fileIndex <= 196; fileIndex++)
      {
      analyzerFileAttributesObjArray[fileIndex] = new
Array();
      analyzerFileAttributesObjArray[fileIndex].file-
Exists = false;
      analyzerFileAttributesObjArray[fileIndex].emp-
tyLines = 0;
      analyzerFileAttributesObjArray[fileIndex].line-
Breaks = 0;
      analyzerFileAttributesObjArray[fileIndex].
joinedLines = 0;
      }
   }


//----------------------------------------------------------
// function getFileList ()
//----------------------------------------------------------
function getFileList ()
   {
```

```
var fileListArray = getFileList();

var fso = new ActiveXObject("Scripting.FileSys-
temObject");

var categoryFolder = fso.GetFolder("./" + paper-
Type);

var fileCollection = new Array();

var fileCollection = new Enumerator(category-
Folder.SubFolders);


for (; !categorySubfolders.atEnd(); categorySub-
folders.moveNext())
    {
    categorySubfoldersCollection[categorySub-
foldersCollection.length] = categorySubfolders.
item().name;
    }
    return categorySubfoldersCollection;
    }


//-----------------------------------------------------------
// function createNonExistingFilesArray()
//-----------------------------------------------------------
function createNonExistingFilesArray()
    {
    nonExistingFilesArrayCurrentIndex = -1;
    var inARun = false;
    nonExistingFilesArray = [];
    nonExistingFilesTabulation = [];
    for (var nonExistingIndex = 1;  nonExistingIndex
<= 196; nonExistingIndex++)
        {
        if (!analyzerFileAttributesObjArray[nonExist-
ingIndex].fileExists)
```

```
        {
        if (inARun)
            {
            nonExistingFilesArray[nonExistingFilesAr-
rayCurrentIndex].highFileNumber++;
            }
        else
            {
            nonExistingFilesArrayCurrentIndex++;

            nonExistingFilesArray[nonExistingFilesAr-
rayCurrentIndex] = new Array();

            nonExistingFilesArray[nonExistingFilesAr-
rayCurrentIndex].lowFileNumber = nonExistingIn-
dex;

            nonExistingFilesArray[nonExistingFilesAr-
rayCurrentIndex].highFileNumber = nonExistingIn-
dex;

            inARun = true;
            }
        }
    else
        {
        inARun = false;
        }
    }


    for (var tabulationIndex = 0; tabulationIndex <=
nonExistingFilesArrayCurrentIndex; tabulationIn-
dex++)
        {
        if (nonExistingFilesArray[tabulationIndex].low-
FileNumber == nonExistingFilesArray[tabulationIn-
dex].highFileNumber)
```

```
        {
            nonExistingFilesTabulation[tabulationIndex]
            = nonExistingFilesArray[tabulationIndex].lowFile-
            Number;

        }
    else
        {
            nonExistingFilesTabulation[tabulationIndex]
            =nonExistingFilesArray[tabulationIndex].lowFile-
            Number + " - " + nonExistingFilesArray[tabula-
            tionIndex].highFileNumber;

        }
    }
}


//----------------------------------------------------------
// function createAnalysisReport ()
//----------------------------------------------------------
function createAnalysisReport ()
  {
  var analysisReportString = "";
//begin full report table
    analysisReportString += "<table cellpadding='5'
cellspacing='0' border='0' style='display:in-
line;padding-left:20px;padding-right:20px-
;padding-top:20px'>";

    analysisReportString += "<tr>";
//begin file summary table
    analysisReportString += "<td colspan='2'
style='text-align:left' ><table cellpadding='0' cell-
spacing='0' border='0' style='padding-top:20px-
;padding-left:20px;padding-right:20px'><tr><t-
d><table cellpadding='0' cellspacing='0'
border='0'>";
```

```
analysisReportString += "<tr>";

analysisReportString += "<td class='bor-
derlessreportitem' style='text-align:left;pad-
ding-right:20px'>Files with Empty Lines: " +
filesWithEmptyLines+ "</td>";

analysisReportString += "<td class='borderless-
reportitem' style='padding-top:5px;padding-bot-
tom:5px;text-align:left'> Existing Files: " + exist-
ingFiles + "</td>";

analysisReportString += "</tr>";

analysisReportString += "<tr>";

analysisReportString += "<td class='borderless-
reportitem' style='text-align:left'>Files with Line
Breaks: " + filesWithLineBreaks + "</td>";

analysisReportString += "<td class='borderless-
reportitem' style='text-align:left'>Missing Files: " +
nonExistingFiles +"</td>";

analysisReportString += "</tr>";

analysisReportString += "<tr>";

analysisReportString += "<td class='borderless-
reportitem' style='padding-top:5px;padding-bot-
tom:5px;text-align:left'> Files with Joined Lines: "
+ filesWithJoinedLines + "</td>";

analysisReportString += "<td></td>";

analysisReportString += "</tr>";
//end file summary table
analysisReportString += "</table></td></tr></
table></td>";

analysisReportString += "</tr>";


analysisReportString += "<tr>";

analysisReportString += "<td colspan='2'
style='height:5px'></td>";

analysisReportString += "</tr>";

analysisReportString += "<tr>";
```

```
//begin files with errors table

analysisReportString += "<td valign='top'
align='center'><table cellpadding='5' cellspac-
ing='0' border='1' class='reportitem' style='dis-
play:inline'>";

analysisReportString += "<tr>";


analysisReportString += "<td colspan='4'
class='reportitem'>Files with errors</td>";

analysisReportString += "</tr>";

analysisReportString += "<tr>";

analysisReportString += "<td rowspan='2'
class='reportitem'>Paper<br>number</td>";

analysisReportString += "<td colspan='4"
class='reportitem'>Error</td>";

analysisReportString += "</tr>";

analysisReportString += "<tr>";

analysisReportString += "<td class='repor-
titem'>Empty<br>line/s</td>";

analysisReportString += "<td class='repor-
titem'>Line<br>break/s</td>";

analysisReportString += "<td class='repor-
titem'>Joined<br>line/s</td>";

analysisReportString += "</tr>";


if (filesWithEmptyLines > 0 || filesWithLineBreaks
> 0 || filesWithJoinedLines > 0)
    {
    for (var errorIndex = 0; errorIndex <= 196;
errorIndex++)
        {
        if (analyzerFileAttributesObjArray[errorIn-
dex].fileExists)
```

```
        {
        if (analyzerFileAttributesObjArray[errorIn-
dex].emptyLines > 0 || analyzerFileAttributesObjA-
rray[errorIndex].lineBreaks > 0 || analyzerFileAttri-
butesObjArray[errorIndex].joinedLines > 0)
            {
            analysisReportString += "<tr>";
            analysisReportString += "<td class='re-
portitem'>" + errorIndex + "</td>";
            if (analyzerFileAttributesObjArray[errorIn-
dex].emptyLines > 0)
                {
                analysisReportString += "<td class='re-
portitem'>" +analyzerFileAttributesObjArray[er-
rorIndex].emptyLines + "</td>";
                }
            else
                {
                analysisReportString += "<td class='re-
portitem'>0</td>";
                }
            if (analyzerFileAttributesObjArray[errorIn-
dex].lineBreaks > 0)
                {
                analysisReportString += "<td class='re-
portitem'>" + analyzerFileAttributesObjArray[er-
rorIndex].lineBreaks + "</td>";
                }
            else
                {
                analysisReportString += "<td class='re-
portitem'>0</td>";
                }
            if (analyzerFileAttributesObjArray[errorIn-
```

```
dex].joinedLines > 0)
        {
            analysisReportString += "<td class='re-
portitem'>" + analyzerFileAttributesObjArray[er-
rorIndex].joinedLines + "</td>";
        }
        else
        {
            analysisReportString += "<td class='re-
portitem'>0</td>";
        }
        }
    }
    }
    else
    {
    analysisReportString += "<tr>";

    analysisReportString += "<td class='repor-
titem'>None</td>";

    analysisReportString += "<td class='repor-
titem'>None</td>";

    analysisReportString += "<td class='repor-
titem'>None</td>";

    analysisReportString += "<td class='repor-
titem'>None</td>";

    analysisReportString += "</tr>";
    }

    analysisReportString += "</tr>";
    analysisReportString += "</table>";
    analysisReportString += "</td>";
```

```
//begin missing files table

analysisReportString += "<td valign='top'
align='center'><table cellpadding='5' cellspac-
ing='0' border='0' class='reportitem' style='dis-
play:inline;margin-left:8px;margin-right:8px'>";

analysisReportString += "<tr>";

analysisReportString += "<td class='repor-
titem'>Missing Files<br>(Paper Number)</td>";

analysisReportString += "</tr>";


if (nonExistingFiles > 0)
  {
  createNonExistingFilesArray();
  for (tabulationIndex = 0; tabulationIndex < non-
ExistingFilesTabulation.length; tabulationIndex++)
    {
    analysisReportString += "<tr><td class='re-
portitem'>" + nonExistingFilesTabulation[tabula-
tionIndex] + "</td></tr>";
    }
  }
  else
  {
  analysisReportString += "<tr><td class='repor-
titem'>None</td></tr>";
  }


analysisReportString += "</tr>";
//end missing files table
analysisReportString += "</table></td>";
//end files with errors table
analysisReportString += "</table></td>";
analysisReportString += "</tr>";
```

```
//end full report table
  analysisReportString += "</table>";
  analyzerDisplayObj.innerHTML = analysisReport-
String;
  }


//-----------------------------------------------------------
// function analyzeInputLine (processingInputLine)
//-----------------------------------------------------------
function analyzeInputLine (processingInputLine)
  {
  if (processingInputLine == null)
    {
    return;
    }
  var inputWorkString = processingInputLine;
  var numberOfSublines = analyzerNumberOfSub-
linesInLine ();

  /*
    if (!firstAnalyzerInputLineHasBeenProcessed)
      {
      inputWorkString = inputWorkString.substr(2,
inputWorkString.length - 2); // 3 for 8 2 for 16
      firstAnalyzerInputLineHasBeenProcessed =
true;
      }
  */

    var closeBracketPos = inputWorkString.index-
Of("]");
  // Remove the line number
```

```
    inputWorkString = inputWorkString.substr(close-
BracketPos + 2, inputWorkString.length - (close-
BracketPos + 1));
  if (inputWorkString.length == 0)
    {
    fileHasEmptyLines = true;
    analyzerFileAttributesObjArray[currentAnalyz-
erPaperNumber].emptyLines++;
    return;
    }
  if (numberOfSublines == 0)
    {
    analyzeSingleLineElement(inputWorkString);
    }
  else
    {
    analyzeMultilineElement(inputWorkString,
numberOfSublines);
    }
  }


//---------------------------------------------------------
// function analyzeSingleLineElement (inputPro-
cessingString)
//---------------------------------------------------------
function analyzeSingleLineElement (inputProcess-
ingString)
  {
  var inputWorkString = inputProcessingString;
  var lineSplitArray = inputWorkString.split(new
RegExp("\{\{\{br\}\}\}", "gi"));
  if (lineSplitArray.length > 1)
    {
```

```
analyzerFileAttributesObjArray[currentAna-
lyzerPaperNumber].lineBreaks += lineSplitArray.
length - 1;
    fileHasLineBreaks = true;
    }
lineSplitArray = inputWorkString.split("@");
if (lineSplitArray.length > 1)
    {
analyzerFileAttributesObjArray[currentAna-
lyzerPaperNumber].joinedLines += lineSplitArray.
length - 1;
    fileHasJoinedLines = true;
    }
}


//------------------------------------------------------------
// function analyzeMultilineElement (inputProcess-
ingString, numberOfSublines)
//------------------------------------------------------------
function analyzeMultilineElement (inputProcess-
ingString, numberOfSublines)
    {
    var inputMultilineString = inputProcessingString;
    var lineSplitArray = inputMultilineString.split(new
RegExp("\{\{\{br\}\}\}", "gi"));
//split the sublines
    var numberOfActualLines = lineSplitArray.length;
    if (numberOfActualLines > numberOfSublines)
        {
analyzerFileAttributesObjArray[currentAna-
lyzerPaperNumber].lineBreaks += numberOfActu-
alLines - numberOfSublines;
    fileHasLineBreaks = true;
```

```
      }
    else if (numberOfActualLines == numberOfSub-
lines - 1)
      {
      analyzerFileAttributesObjArray[currentAnalyz-
erPaperNumber].emptyLines++;
      fileHasEmptyLines = true;
      }
    else if (numberOfActualLines == numberOfSub-
lines - 2)
      {
      analyzerFileAttributesObjArray[currentAnalyz-
erPaperNumber].emptyLines += 2;
      fileHasEmptyLines = true;
      }
    lineSplitArray = inputMultilineString.split("@");
    if (lineSplitArray.length > 1)
      {
      analyzerFileAttributesObjArray[currentAna-
lyzerPaperNumber].joinedLines += lineSplitArray.
length - 1;
      fileHasJoinedLines = true;
      }
    }


//----------------------------------------------------------
// function analyzeFile ()
//----------------------------------------------------------
function analyzeFile ()
  {
  lineMultiplicityErrorArray = [];
  fileHasEmptyLines = false;
```

```
        fileHasLineBreaks = false;

        fileHasJoinedLines = false;

        analyzerInputLineNumber = 0;

        var inputFilePath;

        var fileName;

        fileName = filePath + languageCode + "_" + pap-
    erType + "_p" + zeroedPaperNumber(currentAna-
    lyzerPaperNumber) + ".u16";

        var ForReading = 1

        var fso = new ActiveXObject("Scripting.FileSys-
    temObject");

        var inputFileObject = fso.OpenTextFile(fileName,
    ForReading, false, -1);

        var inputLine;

    //  firstAnalyzerInputLineHasBeenProcessed =
    false;

        while(!inputFileObject.AtEndOfStream)

          {

        inputLine = (inputFileObject.ReadLine());

    // Remember to make duplicate input array if input
    file category is working

          analyzerInputLineNumber++;

          analyzeInputLine(inputLine);

          }

        inputFileObject.close();

        if (fileHasEmptyLines)

          {

        filesWithEmptyLines++;

          }

        if (fileHasLineBreaks)

          {

        filesWithLineBreaks++;
```

```
    }
  if (fileHasJoinedLines)
    {
    filesWithJoinedLines++;
    }
  }


//----------------------------------------------------------
// function analyzeFiles ()
//----------------------------------------------------------
function analyzeFiles ()
  {
  existingFiles = 0;
  nonExistingFiles = 0;
  filesWithEmptyLines = 0;
  filesWithLineBreaks = 0;
  filesWithJoinedLines = 0;
  createBlankFileAttributesArray();
  fillFileAttributesFileExistsFields();
  for (var analyzeIndex = 0; analyzeIndex <=196;
analyzeIndex++)
    {
    if (analyzerFileAttributesObjArray[analyzeIn-
dex].fileExists)
      {
      currentAnalyzerPaperNumber = analyzeIn-
dex;
      analyzeFile(analyzeIndex);
      }
    }
  paperTypeListboxObj.disabled = false;
```

```
      languageCodeListboxObj.disabled = false;
      analyzeButtonObj.disabled = false;
      createAnalysisReport();
      hideWaitBar();
      }


//----------------------------------------------------------------
// function fillFileAttributesFileExistsFields ()
//----------------------------------------------------------------
function fillFileAttributesFileExistsFields ()
  {
  var fileCounter = 0;
  oneOrMoreFilesExist = false;
  for (fileIndex = 0; fileIndex <= 196; fileIndex++)
    {
    if (analyzerFileExists(fileIndex))
      {
      analyzerFileAttributesObjArray[fileIndex].
fileExists = true;
      oneOrMoreFilesExists = true;
      existingFiles++;
      }
    else
      {
      analyzerFileAttributesObjArray[fileIndex].
fileExists = false;
      nonExistingFiles++;
      }
    fileCounter++;
    }
  }
```

```
//------------------------------------------------------------
// function processPaperTypeListboxChange ()
//------------------------------------------------------------
function processPaperTypeListboxChange ()
  {
  var paperTypeSelectedIndex = paperTypeList-
boxObj.selectedIndex;
  paperType = paperTypeListboxObj.options[pap-
erTypeSelectedIndex].value;
  populateLanguageCodeListbox();
  var languageCodeSelectedIndex = language-
CodeListboxObj.selectedIndex;
  languageCode = languageCodeListboxObj.
options[languageCodeSelectedIndex].value;
  filePath = "./" + paperType + "/" + languageCode
+ "/";
  }


//------------------------------------------------------------
// function processLanguageCodeListboxChange ()
//------------------------------------------------------------
function processLanguageCodeListboxChange ()
  {
  var selectedIndex = languageCodeListboxObj.
selectedIndex;
  languageCode = languageCodeListboxObj.
options[selectedIndex].value;
  filePath = "./" + paperType + "/" + languageCode
+ "/";
  }


//------------------------------------------------------------
```

```
// function processAnalyzeButtonClick ()
//----------------------------------------------------------
function processAnalyzeButtonClick ()
  {
  paperTypeListboxObj.disabled = "true";
  languageCodeListboxObj.disabled = "true";
  paperTypeListboxObj.disabled = true;
  languageCodeListboxObj.disabled = true;
  analyzeButtonObj.disabled = true;
  analyzerDisplayObj.innerHTML = "<p
style='font-size:14px;padding-top:11px'>Analyzing
...</p>";
  showWaitBar();
  setTimeout("analyzeFiles()", 500);
  }


//----------------------------------------------------------
// function populateLanguageCodeListbox ()
//----------------------------------------------------------
function populateLanguageCodeListbox ()
  {
  languageCodeListboxObj.options.length = 0;
  languageCodeArray = getLanguageCodeList(pa-
perType);
  if (languageCodeArray.length < 1)
    {
    if (paperType == "reference")
      {
      alert("No reference languages were found in
the ./reference/ directory");
      return;
      }
```

```
    else if (paperType == "working")
      {
      alert("No working languages were found in
the ./working/ directory");
      return;
      }
    }
    for (var languageCodeIndex = 0; languageCo-
deIndex < languageCodeArray.length; languageCo-
deIndex++)
      {
      var newOption = document.createEle-
ment("OPTION");
      newOption.text = languageCodeArray[lan-
guageCodeIndex];
      newOption.value = languageCodeArray[lan-
guageCodeIndex];
      languageCodeListboxObj.add(newOption);
      }
    languageCodeListboxObj.selectedIndex = 0;
    }


//------------------------------------
// function initializeAnalyzer ()
//------------------------------------
function initializeAnalyzer ()
  {
  waitObj = document.getElementById("waitdiv");
  hideWaitBar();
  bodyTagObj = document.getElementById("body-
tag");
  analyzeButtonObj = document.getElementBy-
Id("analyzebutton");
```

```
        paperTypeListboxObj = document.getElementBy-
Id("selectpapertype");

        languageCodeListboxObj = document.getEle-
mentById("selectlanguagecode");

        analyzerDisplayObj = document.getElementBy-
Id("analyzerdisplaydiv");

        analyzerDisplayObj.innerHTML = "";

        populateLanguageCodeListbox();

        processLanguageCodeListboxChange ();
        }
//-------end functions-----
```

ABOUT THE AUTHOR

Troy R. Bishop is an IT professional, who retired after a successful career with the U.S. Bureau of Labor Statistics.

In the BLS Office of Research and Evaluation, he worked alone designing, building, and executing complex software systems requiring innovative design and programming, as requested by mathematical colleagues from around the world who were there on BLS Research Fellowships to research and develop new techniques in mathematics.

Later, in the BLS Office of Technology and Survey Processing, he helped develop large-scale software systems, including the Consumer Price Index (Cost of Living) System and the Locality Pay System (computing salary ranges for every type of formally recognized occupation in the United States at every level of responsibility). While at BLS, he also developed a mainframe computer language and several cutting edge data processing techniques.

Mr. Bishop has been a student and researcher of *The Urantia Book* for nearly half a century. Over that time, he developed various perspectives, which he shares in articles, books, art, and videos, in print and on the internet.

When the text of *The Urantia Book* entered the public domain, on January 1, 2006, he began his first Urantia Book-related programming project, continuing at similar projects until his retirement from those activities.

www.ingramcontent.com/pod-product-compliance
Lightning Source LLC
Chambersburg PA
CBHW071158050326
40689CB00011B/2172